Notes from the

Welcome to a glimpse into the world of international quilting a [...] for you to be able to explore beyond the boundaries of the cou [...] fiber artists are doing.

In many countries, rather than learning from various books, quilters and crafters study under a single master, spending years progressing from simple techniques to the extremely difficult. Intricate designs are celebrated; sewing, embroidery, and quilting by hand is honored; and as such, appliqué, embroidery, and quilting by hand are the typical methods used to quilt.

This book was written in its original language, Japanese, by a master quilter, Yoko Saito. We have done our best to make the directions for each embroidery project easy to understand and fairly easy to figure out if you have some level of quilting experience for the "patchwork embroidery" projects, while maintaining the appearance and intent of the original author and publisher.

We hope the beautifully designed handmade items in this book inspire and encourage you to make them for yourself.

- Important Tips Before You Begin -

The appliqué designs and patterns run from the simple to the more complex. Beginners new to hand piecing, appliqué, and embroidery might choose those patterns with less intricate pieces, while those who are more advanced in appliqué skills should have no difficulty. When it comes to the various projects included in the book, such as the quilted bags, pouches, etc., the following facts might suggest that intermediate or advanced quilters will be more comfortable working on these projects.

- Techniques -

The techniques used in this book are detailed from pages 54~63. This book was specifically created to showcase Ms. Saito's fabric line that celebrates her twentieth year of designing fabric for LECIEN. Swatches of the 20th Centenary Collection are shown on pages 48~51. Ms. Saito continues to delight in designing a number of projects that combine appliqué with patchwork and embroidery. These quilted projects are somewhat more challenging. The project instructions are located on pages 66~111. For these, she assumes that the creator is familiar with sewing, quilting, and bag-making techniques to some degree and thus relies heavily on the creator's ability to figure out the directions that are not specifically written out. It is advisable to read through and understand each project's direction page from beginning to end, including finding the corresponding patterns on the included pattern sheet before beginning.

- Measurements -

The original designs were created using the metric system for dimensions. In order to assist you, we have included the imperial system measurements in brackets. However, please note the samples that appear in the book were created and tested using the metric system. Thus, you will find that if you use the imperial measurements to make the projects, the items you make will not be exactly the same size as when using the metric measurements.

- Patterns/Templates -

Full pattern information for each project appears in several different ways: a) in the materials list, b) in the illustrations and captions, c) in the pattern sheet insert. One must read through all the instructions carefully to understand what size to cut the fabric and related materials, including instructions for each project relating to seam allowances.

- Notions/Accessories -

In this book you will find that some projects will call for a variety of accessories such as zippers, handles, and hardware. While the originals were made with items from Japan, most if not all of the accessories seen have comparable items or are available around the world. However, some of the accessories are available through Yoko Saito's quilt shop in Japan or online. See the copyright page for further information.

Stitch Publications, 2016

Yoko Saito's

Quilts & Projects
from my Favorite Fabrics

Centenary Collection by Yoko Saito

Featuring the 20th Anniversary Centenary Collection by LECIEN

Introduction

The selection of fabric for any quilt or patchwork project is essential to the success of the finished items. Twenty years ago it was difficult to find quilting cotton with the specific colors that I was looking for in Japan. It was then that a fabric manufacturer contacted me to see if I would be interested in designing an original line of quilting fabric for them. Immediately my mind went to the concept of replicating the look of fabrics that I had seen in antique quilts. Over the years I had collected books on antique quilts and had taken quite a few pictures during my travels. I used a magnifying glass to examine and study the general colors and types of patterns that were often used. I began to draw my own unique designs and chose colors that reflected my favorite antique quilts. The fabric line became known as the Centenary Collection.

It is hard to believe that twenty years have passed, and I have finished my twentieth collection with Lecien. As is true with everyone, I believe, my own color choices have changed and grown over the years. The early years reflected colors that are often identified with the warmth of Americana or American country, while in the last few years I have found a love for the cool, smoky shades of the Scandinavian region. Even now, however, I feel that I continue to evolve in my love and understanding of color.

Color choice and the patterns on the fabric are at the heart of patchwork and quilting that most speak to me. In fact, it is perhaps the most important part of my process and the driving force in designing over the years in all my work. The finished fabric is the culmination of combining the color and the pattern.

Unfortunately for all of us, fabrics that we love or see are not available forever and are sometimes hard to find. Most of the fabrics used in the quilts and patchwork projects in this book are from my Centenary Collection released in the fall of 2014 to specifically celebrate the many years I've been designing. If you desire to replicate these designs to my finished works and can't find the fabric from this collection, I encourage you to do what I did for many years. Study the designs and colors of the fabric you are trying to recreate and look for one that matches as closely as possible. This will make your finished project even more of a reflection of you.

Yoko Saito

Contents

Flower Shoulder Bag

Instructions – p.66

*The soft, pale tones are calming as the colors and fabrics of both the appliqué and embroidery bring
out the subtleties of the yarn-dyed woven used for the main fabric of the bag.*

The detailed red star makes a bold statement against the background fabric. The
random white color from the red fabric gives the eye another level of interest.

3 Blue Star Bag

Instructions – p.70

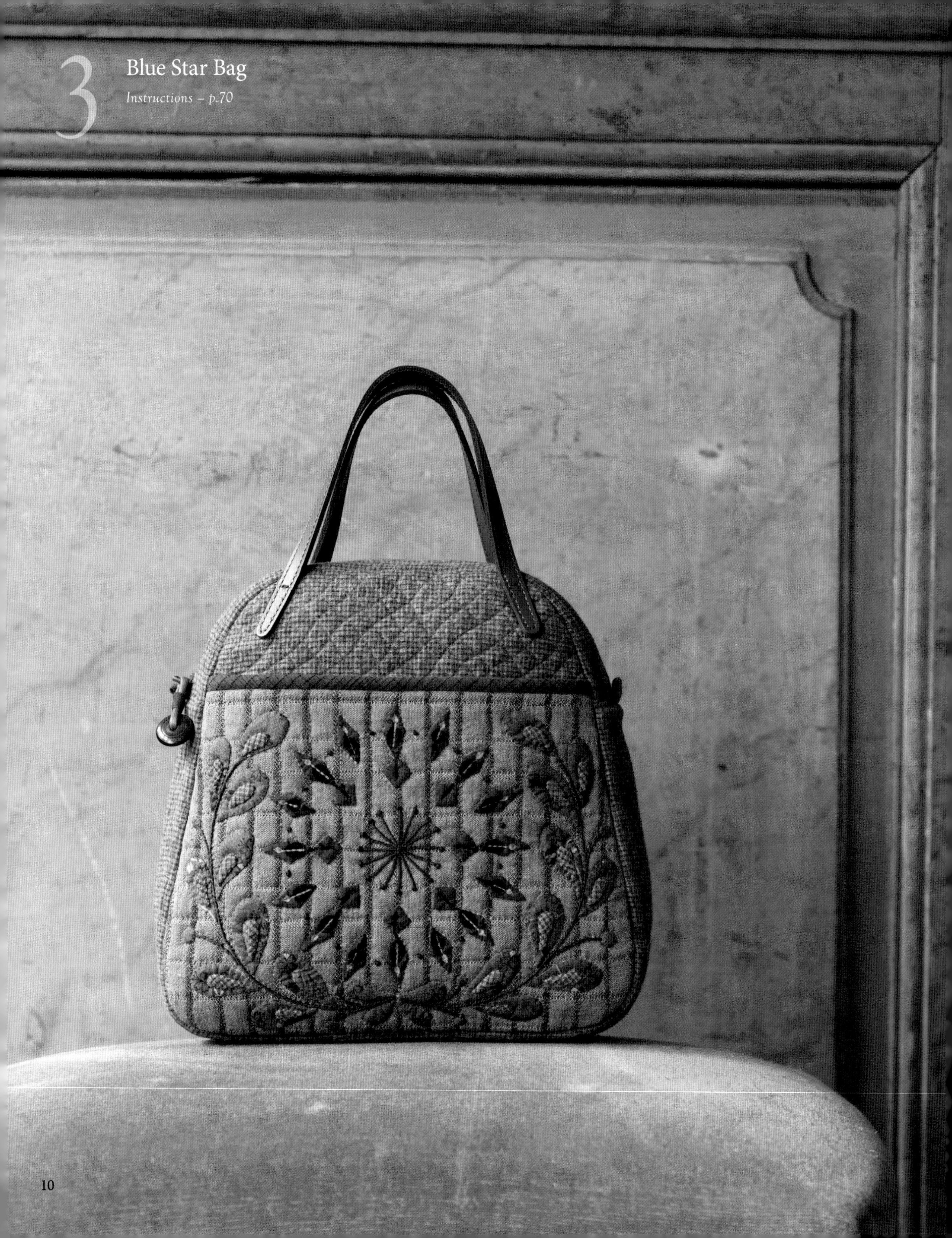

A beautiful symmetrical star pattern is created by repeating the appliqué and embroidery in a radius to create a circle.

4

Little Birds
Shoulder Bag

Instructions – p.72

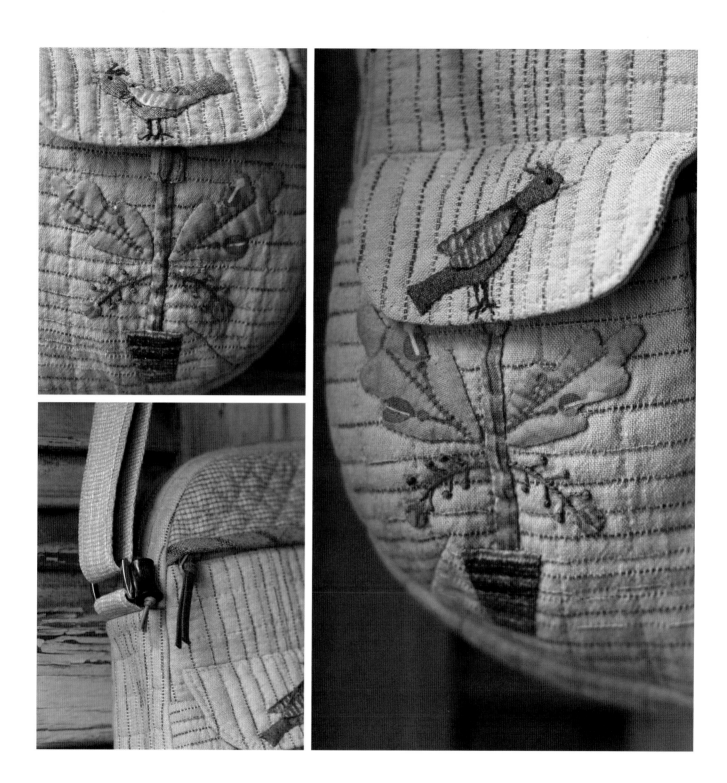

Two little birds face each other happily on this shoulder bag with plenty of pockets.

Leaves Galore Granny Bag

Instructions – p.74

Leaves in a variety of colors are appliquéd and embroidered along the vertical piping in the bag design which is used to resemble the main branches of a tree. The wrong side of the fabric is used for the background in order to get a softer look.

This unique looking bag keeps its shape by using heavyweight fusible interfacing. It is particularly pleasing to add appliqué to the gussets as well as the front flap.

These are adorable little pouches with handles that cleverly use only one side of a zipper tape in order to lessen bulky seams.

9 Owl Bag
Instructions – p.80

The wise old owl is a charming figure in the forest. The main fabrics used for the bag and the quilting reflect the forest, trees, and plants.

20th Anniversary   CENTENARY COLLECTION   BY YOKO SAITO & LECIE

Woodgrain prints are very useful as is seen in the basketweave and handle of the tote as well as the soil from which the mini flowers are growing on the pouch.

Using the repeated dot and cross combination to create an all over design for this bag is anything but monotonous when you use a variety of colors and fabric choices.

13

Spinning Circles
Shoulder Bag

Instructions – p.88

Cutting up and combining sections of two different blocks to make circles creates the illusion that they are spinning.

14

Pieced Blocks
Shoulder Bag

Instructions – p.90

*Piecing each of the blocks using narrow strips of the same fabric is
more interesting to the eye than using a solid piece.*

Patchwork
Pencil Case

Instructions – p.92

*Creating your own patchwork fabric out of many small miscellaneous
scraps can be a lot of fun as you can see from this pencil case.*

The button closure on this pouchette adds to the charming silhouette.

The tablecloth, placemats, and tea cozy all speak to the appeal of houses and buildings in patchwork. The low contrast of color works particularly well for the border of the tablecloth.

21·22 Fabric Boxes (1 & 2)
Instructions – p.100

Storage boxes to hold the fabric for projects are fun to make. Sew together fabric strips or scraps to create the outside of the boxes. You can always sew these together by machine if you are not someone who loves to sew by hand.

Scissors Holder
Instructions – p.102

Sewing Case
Instructions – p.104

Hexagon Pincushion
Instructions – p.79

It is easier to work when your sewing area is organized by having specific places to keep your various tools and notions.
Appliqué the items that go inside on the outside of the bag to help you remember what goes where.

The contrast between the rustic floral arrangements in baskets appliquéd against a light toile background fabric makes for a lovely wall hanging.

An arrangement of different sizes of the traditional Bethlehem Star blocks make up this twinkling quilt.

Swaying Flowers Quilt

Instructions – p.109

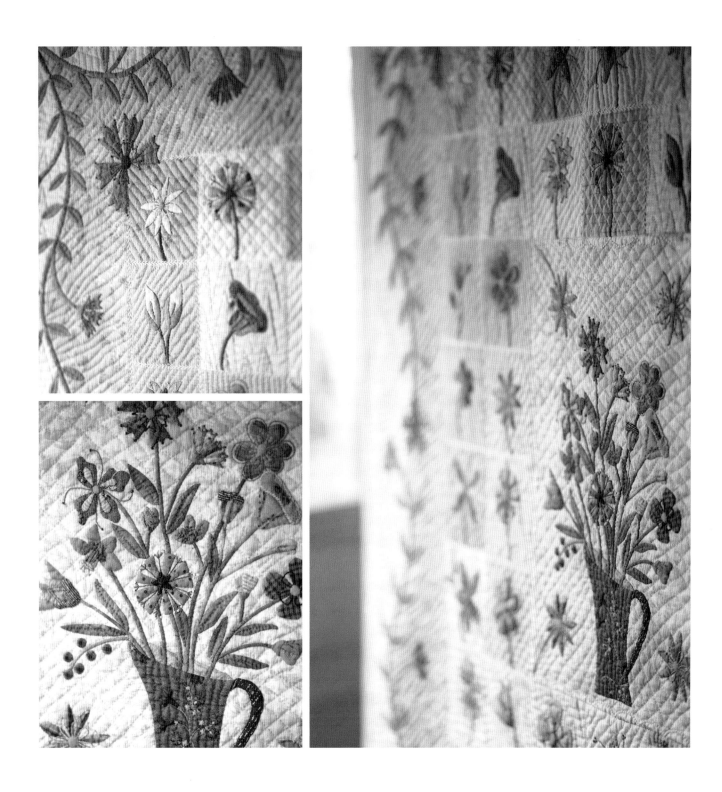

Each of the appliquéd flowers has movement as though it is swaying in the wind. Make your quilting follow the motifs for a stunning finished quilt.

Introducing the 20th Centenary Collection

Fall of 2014

No.30910 Grain Kernels

No.30916 Toile

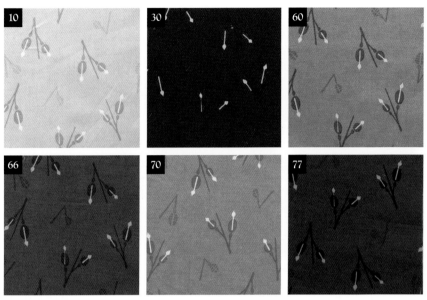

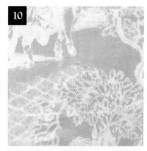

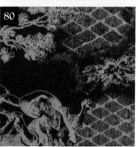

This pattern is a slightly modern take on two kernels of grain scattered across the fabric. Color numbers 30, 66, and 77 would be perfect as primary fabrics in any given project.

No.30914 Wood Grain

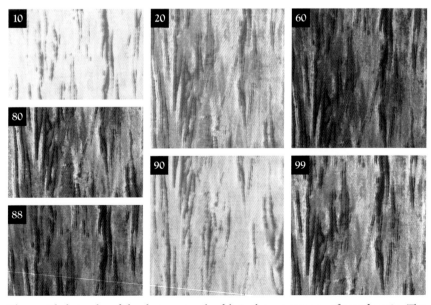

The mottled streaks of the design give the fabric the appearance of wood grain. The way I used color and shading also gives it a three-dimensional look.

I designed a toile de jouy-like pattern reminiscent of the fabric originated in France in the late 1700's that can be used in a variety of ways in the projects.

No.30913 Arrowheads

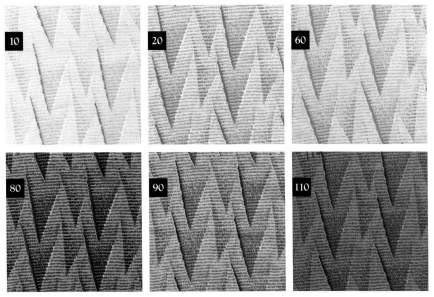

While the design shows a representation of movement, the overall pattern of the arrowheads is not so distinct that it can't be used for a background fabric.

No.30911 Flowers & Tendrils

This all-over pattern of flowers and tendrils has a three-dimensional depth to it and is useful in the rich color ways that are available.

No.30912 Dots & Streaks

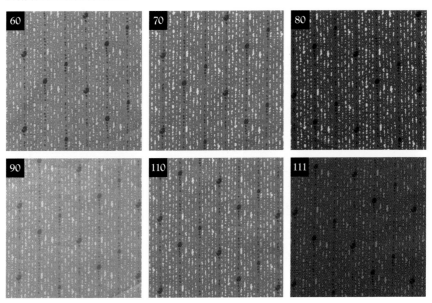

The indistinct dots and irregular stripes make this fabric interesting for vertical or horizontal applications.

No.30917 Brushed Flannel Plaid

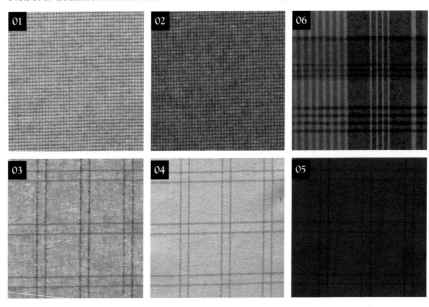

I happen to love to use brushed flannel in my projects and mix them in with other cottons. The brushing of the fibers softens the lines in the pattern and give them a warmth. If you are not a fan of brushed flannels, you can use the wrong side facing out.

No.30915 Plaid

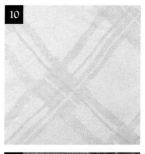

The soft diagonal lines of the pattern give a soft hand-drawn appearance. This design is perhaps best used in a background or base fabric.

No.30918 Yarn-dyed Wovens

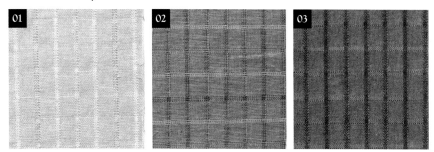

No.30919 Yarn-dyed Wovens

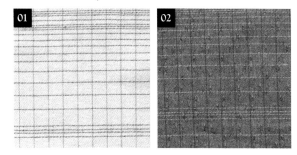

No.30920 Yarn-dyed Wovens

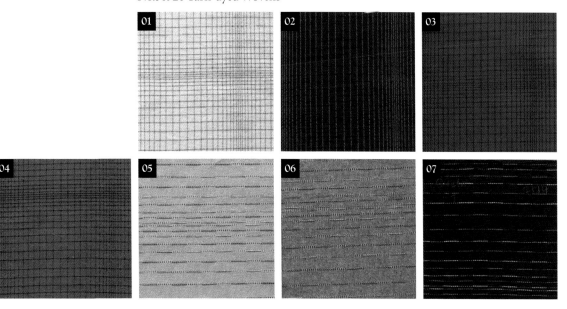

Yarn-dyed woven fabrics are not a requirement when making my quilts or bags. I designed these to coordinate with the entire collection. Play with using either the right or wrong side of the fabric to get different looks.

Quiltmaking Basics

The following is a list of basic tools and notions that are useful to have on hand for making quilts.

Essential Quilting Notions & Tools

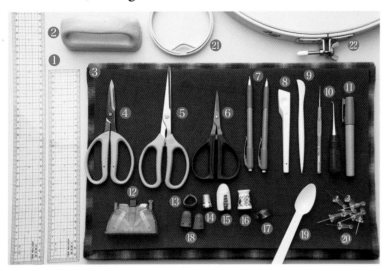

❶ Ruler - Used to trace straight lines when transferring patterns. Rulers with markings made for quilters are useful.

❷ Weights (paperweights, beanbags, etc.) - Used to weigh down a small quilt when quilting.

❸ Non-Slip Board - The non-slip surface board is used when marking fabric or when using the fabric pressing tool to turn under the seam allowances. The soft side backed with batting and fabric can be used as a mini ironing surface.

❹ Scissors (a pair specifically for paper) - They will last longer if each pair is used for specific things, such as for paper, fabric, or thread.

❺ Scissors (a pair specifically for fabric).

❻ Scissors (a pair specifically for thread).

❼ Marking Pencil - Used to transfer patterns to either paper or fabric or for marking quilting lines. Mechanical pencils allow for greater precision and lines disappear with water.

❽ Seam Pressing Tool - Used to press seam allowances down, in lieu of ironing.

❾ Appliqué Hera Marker - Used when working with appliqué pieces. The curved area is particularly useful.

❿ Awl - To mark corner points when transferring and drawing patterns or to punch holes into leather or suede.

⓫ Glue Stick- Used to temporarily hold fabric in place in lieu of pins or basting.

⓬ Needle Threader - A simple tool making it easier to thread needles.

⓭ Adjustable Thimble - To help push the needle and thread through thick sections when quilting.

⓮ Metal Thimble - Used to push the needle through the cloth when quilting. (Flat and Round Head).

⓯ Leather Thimble - Slip this over a metal thimble on your middle finger as you work to keep work from slipping.

⓰ Porcelain Thimble - Useful and beautiful, once you get used to it.

⓱ Ring Cutter - Conveniently worn on your left (or right) thumb and used for cutting threads as you are working.

⓲ Rubber Thimbles - Wear on your right index finger during quilting or appliqué to help grab the needle and reduce slippage.

⓳ Spoon - Often used when pin-basting a quilt. Diaper pins are easy to use for this method.

⓴ Push Pins - Useful to keep layers from shifting when getting ready to baste the quilting sandwich. The longer the pin, the better.

㉑ Embroidery Hoop - Used to secure fabric when doing embroidery.

㉒ Quilting Hoop - Used for any projects that are too small to fit on a quilting frame or require to be held by hand while quilting.

Pins & Needles

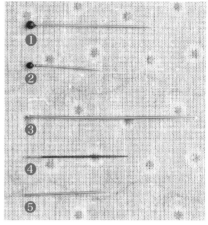

❶ Straight Pins - An easy-to-use longer straight pin with a small head.

❷ Appliqué Pins - A short pin, with a small head that won't get in the way while you appliqué.

❸ Basting Needle - A long needle used for basting.

❹ Appliqué or Piecing Needle - Easy to appliqué with, as they tend to bend with use. Used to piece together fabric.

❺ Quilting Betweens Needles - Shorter than sharps, used for quilting.

Thread

❶ Basting Thread - Used for basting.

❷ Sewing Thread - Used for piecing or stitching; appropriate for either hand sewing or machine sewing.

❸ Quilting Thread - A coated, durable thread used for hand-quilting that is slightly thicker. Use shades of thread that closely match the fabric color.

*Other notions and tools I use include the following: quilt stand (used when quilting large projects), heavyweight paper (for templates/ patterns), tracing paper, light table, cellophane tape, iron, and spray adhesive.

Basic Quilting Terminology

Thimble Placement

See the photo above for proper finger placement of quilting thimbles and ring cutter so as not to hurt your fingers while you quilt. There are many thimbles on the market, so find ones that are most comfortable for you while you work.

If you are right-handed, you will quilt with your right hand using your thumb, index and middle fingers. The middle finger will be used to push the needle through and will be protected by a metal thimble covered by a leather thimble. You may also use a porcelain thimble fitted with a rubber thimble underneath so it does not slip. The index finger will be fitted with a rubber thimble to help grasp the needle securely to pull it through the layers of the quilt. The ring cutter should be placed on the thumb.

For those who are left-handed, the process is basically the same but on opposite hands.

- **Sewing Marks** - marks that are placed on fabric with fabric marking pencils to help line up pieces when sewing.
- **Appliqué** - cutting and applying pieces of fabric to another background fabric to create designs.
- **Quilting Facing** - fabric (often muslin) used against the back of batting when quilting the top to create the back layer of the quilt sandwich. Most often used when not wanting the quilting from the front to show through on the lining or backing.
- **English Paper Piecing** - hand-sewing pieces of fabric around paper templates, then sewing the edges together to piece.
- **Backing/Lining** - fabric that is used for the back side of a quilt, bag, or other project.
- **Stitch-in-the-Ditch Quilting** - quilting in the seam lines of a quilt or a hair's width outside of an appliqué.
- **Quilt Top** - pieces that make up the front of a quilt or quilted project. Often made up of pieced or appliquéd quilt blocks.
- **Backstitch** - the backstitch makes a very strong seam when sewing by hand.
- **Pinwheel Pressing** - pressing seam allowances that are overlapping in one direction.
- **Pressing on the Fold** - pressing fabric with the fold just covering the seam.
- **Quilting** - enclosing a warm layer of batting between two layers of fabric and kept in place by lines of stitching.
- **Batting** - a layer of insulation that lies between the top and backing/lining of a quilt or quilted project. Often made of cotton, wool, bamboo or other fabrics, batting can be fairly thin or very lofty.
- **Running Stitch** - the simplest of stitches to join two pieces of cloth.
- **Bag Opening/Zipper Opening Fabrics** - the fabric used at the top opening edge of a bag or the zipper opening of a project. The fabric used is often a contrasting fabric.
- **Basting** - sewing loose, large running stitches to hold two or more pieces of fabric together temporarily.
- **Fusible Batting** - interior quilt insulation that has single or double-sided adhesive that will stick to the fabric when heated by an iron.
- **Fusible Interfacing** - an adhesive-sided

material of varying weights that gives additional shape, strength, or support to fabric when heated with an iron.
- **Cut-to-Size** - cutting pieces of fabric for a pattern with no added seam allowance.
- **Pleat** - fabric that is folded back on itself; pressed, and sewn in place along the seam line or edge.
- **Zipper Tabs/Tabs** - tabs sewn onto a pouch or bag at either end of a zipper or bag opening. Easy to grab hold, they aid in opening and closing the bag or zipper.
- **Knotting Thread** - small knots that are made at the beginning and end of sewing to secure the thread and seams in place.
- **Background Fabric** - fabric upon which appliqué or embroidery is done.
- **Right Sides Together** - sewing two pieces of fabric with the printed or outer ("right") side of the fabric laid against each other.
- **End-to-End Sewing** - sewing from one edge of the piece to the other.
- **Seam Allowance** - the extra amount of fabric between the edge and the seam when two pieces of fabric are being sewn together.
- **Mark-to-Mark Sewing** - sewing between the seam allowance marks.
- **Binding** a cover for raw edges using a folded and stitched-down width of fabric on both the front and back. Most often made of bias fabric.
- **Pattern** - the drawn designs that make up the quilt top or project.
- **Piece** - shaped pieces of fabric that will be stitched together; often triangular, square, and diamond shapes.
- **Piecing** - sewing fabric pieces (triangles, squares, etc.) together to create segments or blocks for a quilt top.
- **Border** - a strip or strips of fabric that border the center design of a quilt in order to frame it.
- **Overlock Sewing** - sewing over the edge of one or more pieces for edging, hemming or seaming.
- **Gusset** - adding a piece of fabric, or sewing seams into fabric to add breadth and provide expansion. Often used when making quilted bags and pouches.
- **Facing** - fabric used for reinforcement, such as around bag openings.

⋯⋯ *p.18 - A full-size template/pattern is on Side A of the pattern sheet insert.*

Follow the step-by-step instructions below to learn how to make this coffee cup pouch. Techniques shown are piecework, appliqué, bias binding application, basting, quilting, finishing seams, and sewing in a zipper.

▶ Materials Needed

Assorted fat quarters or scraps (piecing, bottom)
Cotton print - (pouch opening appliqué)
 - 10 × 30 cm [4" × 11¾"]
Muslin (pouch bottom) - 8 × 8 cm [3⅛" × 3⅛"]
Homespun (handle) - 25 × 15 cm [9¾" × 5⅞"]
Batting - 45 × 20 cm [17¾" × 7⅞"]
Homespun - (pouch lining) - 45 × 20 cm [17¾" × 7⅞"]
Homespun (decorative bias strip) - 1.1 × 30 cm [½" × 11¾"]
Fusible interfacing (bottom, handle) - 10 × 20 cm [4" × 7⅞"]
Homespun (zipper tab) - 3 × 8 cm [1¼" × 3⅛"]
1 Zipper - 30 cm (11¾")

Dimensional Diagram

Pouch Body

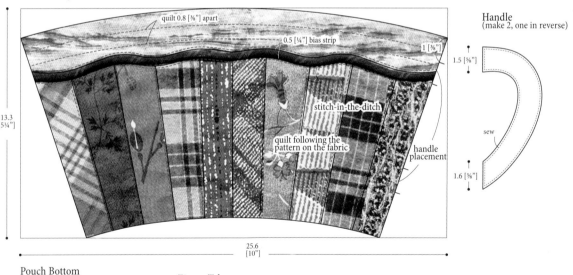

Handle
(make 2, one in reverse)

Pouch Bottom

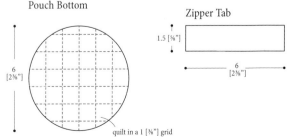

Zipper Tab

Piecing the Pouch Body

0.7 [¼"] seam allowance

1
Choose ten different scraps for the pieced pouch body. Place the paper template copied from the pattern sheet insert on the wrong side of each scrap of fabric and trace around the template using a marking pencil. Cut the piece out adding 0.7 cm [¼"] for the seam allowance.

2
Line the ten pieces up in the order you want them to be sewn together. You will begin to piece them together starting from the left side.

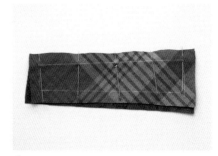

3
Pick up the first two pieces and with right sides together, align the finished sewing lines. Use straight pins to pin the two pieces together at each end, in the center and in the spaces between.

0.5 [¼"]

4
Begin stitching 0.5 cm [¼"] from the outside edge along the finished sewing line. Take one backstitch to secure the end point.

finished sewing line

5
Use a running stitch to sew along the marked finished sewing lines.

0.5 [¼"]

6
Sew to within 0.5 cm [¼"] of the end and take a single backstitch to secure the stitching; cut off the thread leaving a little tail.

0.7 [¼"]

7
These two pieces of fabric are now sewn together and the sub-section is complete.

8
Always take the time to trim the seam allowance down to an exact 0.7 cm [¼"] for neat and beautiful seams.

9
When hand-piecing, fold the finished seam to one side and press, leaving 0.1 cm [¹/₁₆"] showing over fold. This will hide the actual seam on the right side for a neater appearance.

10

Lay the sub-section on top of a non-slip board with right side up. Using the seam pressing tool, press down firmly along the handsewn seam.

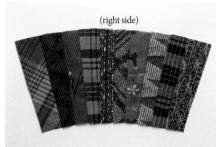

(right side)

(wrong side)

11

Repeat steps 3-10, continuing to sew the pieces together from left to right. Press all the seam allowances in the same direction as you work.

12

Place the paper template for the pouch body copied from the pattern sheet insert on the right side of the pieced fabric (note that the template is only ½ of the whole; you will need to place this on the fold to get the entire template for the pouch body); trace around the template using a marking pencil.

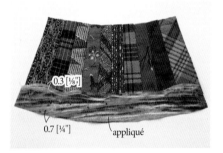

0.3 [⅛"]

0.7 [¼"]   appliqué

13

Place the paper template for the pouch opening copied from the pattern sheet insert on the right side of the pieced fabric (cut this template on the fold also); trace around the template using a marking pencil. Cut out the opening piece with a 0.3 cm [⅛"] seam allowance along the wavy edge and a 0.7 cm [¼"] on the remaining three sides.

14

Turn the raw edges along the wavy edge under 0.3 cm [⅛"] along the marked finished sewing line.

Using tiny straight pins made specifically for detailed appliqué work is recommended.

15

Using the blindstitch, take a tiny backstitch to secure then begin to blind stitch along the wavy edge.

finished sewing line

0.1 [¹/₁₆"] seam allowance

16

Make tiny snips 0.1 cm [¹/₁₆"] from the finished sewing line wherever there is an inside (concave) curve to help with ease.

17

Turn the seam allowance under with the tip of the needle as you blindstitch. Take two very tiny stitches at the points where you snipped the fabric to secure these areas.

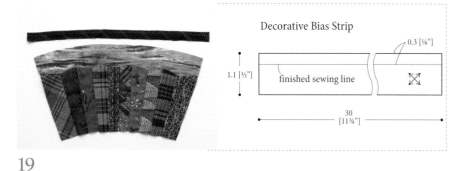

Decorative Bias Strip

0.3 [⅛"]

1.1 [½"]

finished sewing line

30
[11¾"]

18

The appliquéd pouch opening is complete.

19

Cut the bias strip 1.1 × 30 cm [½" × 11¾"] long. Use a marking pencil to draw a 0.3 cm [⅛"] seam along on the wrong side of only one edge (note that the seam allowances will both end up being 0.3 cm [⅛"] while the finished decorative bias showing will be 0.5 cm [¼"]).

0.1 [¹⁄₁₆"]

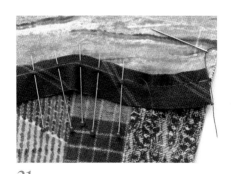

20

Pin the bias strip with right sides together against the pouch body, inserting the pin through the finished sewing line and into the pouch body 0.1 cm [¹⁄₁₆"] from the appliquéd wavy edge of the pouch opening as shown.

21

Pin the bias strip to the pouch body using as many pins as necessary to align the fabrics. Mark a backstitch at the beginning and continue to sew along the finished sewing line using a running stitch.

22

As you did in step 17, when you reach the areas where the seam allowance has been snipped in the concave areas of the pouch opening, take two tiny backstitches to secure the seam allowance.

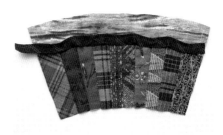

0.5 [¼"]

23

One side of the decorative bias strip is complete.

24

Flip the bias strip up along the finished sewing line; finger press. Use your needle to turn 0.3 cm [⅛"] of the edge under, leaving 0.5 cm [¼"] showing on the front. Pin in place; blindstitch down to the pouch opening.

25

The entire pouch body front top is now complete.

Basting the Pouch Body

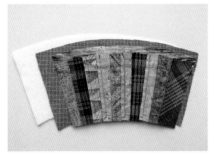

1

Cut both the lining fabric and the batting with generous 2 cm [¾"] seam allowance on both sides and a 0.7 cm [¼"] seam allowance on the top and bottom. Layer them in the following order: batting, lining, and pieced pouch body (with right sides together).

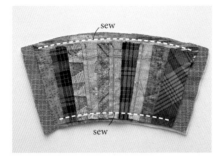

2

The seam allowances for the top and bottom of all pieces should be 0.7 cm [¼"]. Sew across the top and bottom from side to side between marks.

3

Trim the batting down right next to the stitching on both the top and bottom.

4

Take four snips equal distances apart into the seam allowance 0.1 cm [¹/₁₆"] away from the stitching along the curved bottom edge.

5

Turn the piece right side out. Use an iron to press the pouch body into shape.

6

Lay the pouch body sandwich on a board or carpet, securing the edges with push pins. It is best to do the basting steps while it is secured down and not while being held in your hand as it is too easy for it to get wrinkled as you work.

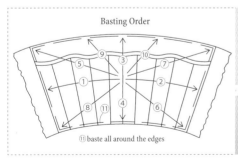

7

Starting in the center of the pouch body with a length of knotted thread, baste all the way to the left edge. Use a spoon to help lift the needle from the surface as you baste. Knot the thread at the edge and cut it, leaving a 2-3 cm [¾" - 1¼ "] tail. Repeat basting from the center out in a sunburst pattern following the order in the illustration above.

8

Your basted quilt sandwich should look like this when you are done. I often use contrasting thread color to make it easier to see when I pull them out after I finish the quilting.

Quilting the Pouch Body

For quilts that are too small to fit into a quilting hoop, you must make adjustments. Using the non-slip board and weights, place the quilt as shown to keep it from moving while you work. Always start in the center of your quilt sandwich and work your way out toward the edges.

You can either mark a quilting design on your quilt top or choose to quilt any pattern desired. I often like to quilt using the pattern that is on the fabric.

1

Knot the end of the thread and insert the needle into the quilt top and batting about 1 cm [⅜"] away from where you will begin the first stitch. Pull the thread through until the knot is lying on the surface of the quilt top. Gently tug the thread to pop the knot through the quilt top to bury it in the batting.

2

Before you begin quilting, take one little stitch without going all the way through to the backing.

3

Insert the needle again at the first stitch perpendicular to the top and pull through the back, coming up very close to the first stitch. Insert the needle down again with your right hand until you feel the tip of the needle with your left finger under the quilt and immediately come back up.

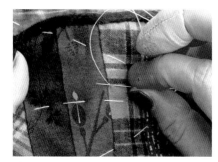

4

Repeat this rocking motion until you have several stitches on your needle. Then use the thimble to push the needle through the quilt. Pull the thread to even the tension. Repeat until the end of your quilting line.

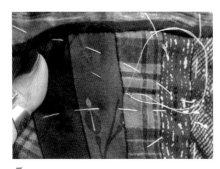

5

When you reach the end of your quilting line, backstitch into the preceding space, bringing the needle up to create the final stitch.

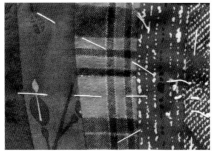

6

Insert the needle into the last stitch again and work the needle through the batting, bringing the tip of the needle out about 1 cm [⅜"] away from the last stitch. Carefully cut the thread close to the quilt top.

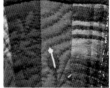

Sewing in the Zipper

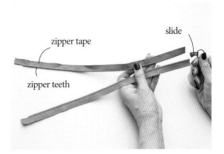

1

Cut off the bottom stop at the end of the zipper. Remove the slide and separate the zipper into two pieces. For this project, we will only use one side of the zipper.

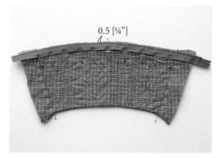

2

Place the pouch body with the lining side up. Place pins on either end to mark the finished sewing lines of the sides as well as the center point along the top edge.

3

Find the center point of the zipper tape; align the zipper tape to the center point on the pouch body. Pin along the sewing line, which should be 0.5 cm [¼"] away from the teeth and the pouch opening edge.

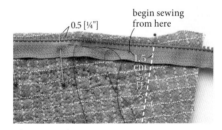

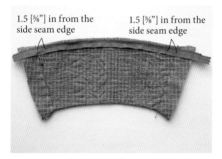

4

Use a backstitch to sew the zipper tape to the pouch body. Start sewing 1.5 cm [⅝"] in from the marked side seam edge.

5

You should be able to sew the zipper in without drawing a finished sewing line by eyeing the 0.5 cm [¼"] distance from the edge of the teeth down. As you sew, make sure that your needle is only going through to the batting and not through to the front side so that the stitches won't show.

6

End your sewing 1.5 cm [⅝"] in from the other marked side seam edge.

7

Blindstitch the edge of the tape, catching only the lining fabric as you sew.

8

With right sides together, fold the pouch body, aligning the marked finished sewing lines of the side seams; pin. Pin the ends of the zipper out of the way on both sides.

9

If you are using a sewing machine, set your stitch length to 0.2 cm [¹/₁₆"] and sew the side seam. Use a backstitch if you are sewing the seam by hand.

10

Choose one side of the lining seam allowance to use to bind the raw edges; fold out of the way. Trim the rest of the seam allowances down to 0.7 cm [¼"].

11

Fold the lining seam allowance over the raw edges; use an awl to push the fabric under tightly and neatly. Use pins to secure the bound seam in place.

12

Use a ladder stitch to sew up the bound side seam.

13

The side seam of the pouch body is complete.

14

Unpin the ends of the zipper. Align the ends of the teeth and cut off both ends just under the zipper stop. This will make it easier for the slide to go back on.

15

Holding the zipper teeth together, thread the zipper slide back onto the teeth. Remember that the pouch is still inside out, so the slide should be upside down and going in the correct direction.

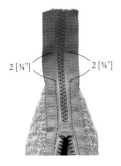

16

With the zipper partially closed, measure 2 cm [¾"] past the side seam and make a mark on the zipper tape.

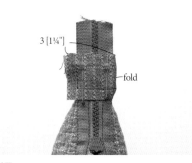

17

Using the 3 × 8 cm [1¼" × 3⅛"] fabric for the zipper tab, cut out a piece that is 1.5 × 6 cm [⅝" × 2⅜"] with 0.7 cm [¼"] seam allowances. With right sides together, fold the zipper tab in half width-wise.

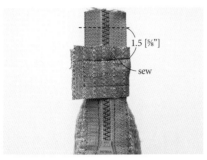

18

Use a sewing machine to sew across the end away from the pouch. Trim off the end of the zipper leaving 1.5 cm [⅝"].

19

Turn the zipper tab right side out, covering the cut end of the zipper. Turn the seam allowances under to exactly cover the zipper tape.

20

Machine stitch around the edges of the zipper tab.

Sewing on the Pouch Bottom and Handle

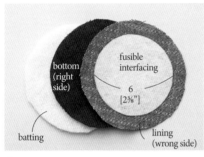

1

Cut a 6 cm [2 ⅜"] circle from the fusible interfacing. Cut 6 cm [2 ⅜"] circles with 0.7 cm [¼"] seam allowance from the batting, bottom fabric, and bottom lining. Iron the fusible interfacing to the wrong side of the lining; layer as shown above.

2

Sew around the circle on the finished sewing line leaving 5 cm [2"] open for turning. Trim the batting close to the stitching line.

3

Sew a running stitch within the seam allowance around the circle except for where you will turn the circle right side out. Pull the thread up to gather the seam allowance toward the center; tie off.

4

Turn the pouch bottom right side out; finger shape into a circle. Blindstitch the opening closed.

5

Machine quilt the pouch bottom in a 1 cm [⅜"] grid. The pouch bottom is complete.

6

With wrong sides together, pin the pouch body to the pouch bottom. Use a ladder stitch and very small stitches to sew the two pieces together. Be careful to only pick up the fabric on the outside (not the lining) so that the stitches don't show through.

7

The pouch body is complete.

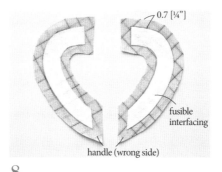

0.7 [¼"]

fusible interfacing

handle (wrong side)

8

Cut two pieces of fusible interfacing and two pieces of fabric for the handle that mirror each other, adding 0.7 cm [¼"] seam allowance to the fabric pieces. Fuse the interfacing to the wrong sides of the fabric.

9

With sharp scissors snip into the inner curve of the handle approximately every 0.7 cm [¼"]. Using a fabric glue stick, run a line of glue along the inner curve edge of the piece.

10

Using a stylus or your fingers, fold the snipped seam allowance toward the glue and press down. This allows you to get a beautiful curve.

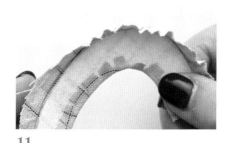

11

Sew a running stitch within the seam allowance around the outer edge of the handle. Pull the thread up gently to gather the seam allowance toward the center.

12

Fold the seam allowance at the end in and cut off the dog ear to lessen the amount of fabric to turn under. Fold the side seam over neatly, being careful to keep the edges from showing on the right side.

13

This completes one side of the handle. Make the remaining mirror image following the same steps.

14

Machine stitch around the outer handle edges with wrong sides together. Use a ladder stitch to sew the pieces together if you choose to hand-sew them.

15

Pin the handle in place on the side of the pouch body. Blindstitch the handle ends to the body with tiny stitches to secure. This completes the pouch.

LECIEN

20th Anniversary
Centenary Collection

by Yoko Saito & LECIEN

Projects

- All measurements listed for the following projects are in centimeters (cm) and in inches [in brackets].

- Seam allowances should be 0.7 cm [¼"] for all piecing unless otherwise specified. Seam allowances for appliqué pieces should be 0.3 cm [⅛"]. Seam allowances must be added to the patterns.

- The dimensions of the finished project are shown in the drawings.

- Note that the quilted pieces tend to shrink somewhat, depending on the type of fabric used, the thickness of the batting, the amount of quilting, and individual quilting technique.

- For portions of the handbags, as well as the quilting, a sewing machine may be used. However, all the projects can be made by hand.

1 Flower Shoulder Bag ------- *p.06* (full-size template/pattern - Side A of the pattern sheet insert)

► **Materials Needed**

Assorted fat quarters or scraps (appliqué)
Homespun (bag body, handle/gusset)
 - 110×40 cm [43¼" × 15¾"]
Homespun (bag opening, handle/gusset lining)
 - 80×20 cm [31½" × 7⅞"]
Cotton print (lining)
 - 110×60 cm [43¼" × 23⅝"]
Batting
 - 110×40 cm [43¼" × 15¾"]
Cotton print (bias binding)
 - 2.5×160 cm [1" ×63"]
Fusible interfacing

 - 110×35 cm [43¼" × 13¾"]
Lightweight fusible interfacing
 - 45×10 cm [17¾" × 4"]
1 Zipper - 30 cm [11¾"]
Embroidery floss - colors as desired
Wooden beads
Waxed cord (zipper pull)

► **Instructions**

1. Using the diagram below and the pattern, piece, appliqué, and embroider the bag body front and back.
2. With right sides together and batting on the back, sew the top seam. Turn right side out; baste together the three layers; quilt and sew darts.
3. Make the handle/gusset. Sew the bag body front, back, and handle gusset together; bind raw edges.
4. Make the bag opening.
5. With right sides together, sew the bag opening and the handle underside facing together. Align this to the bag body with wrong sides together; blindstitch the bag opening and handle underside facing to the bag body and handle.
6. Make the zipper pull and attach it to the zipper clasp.

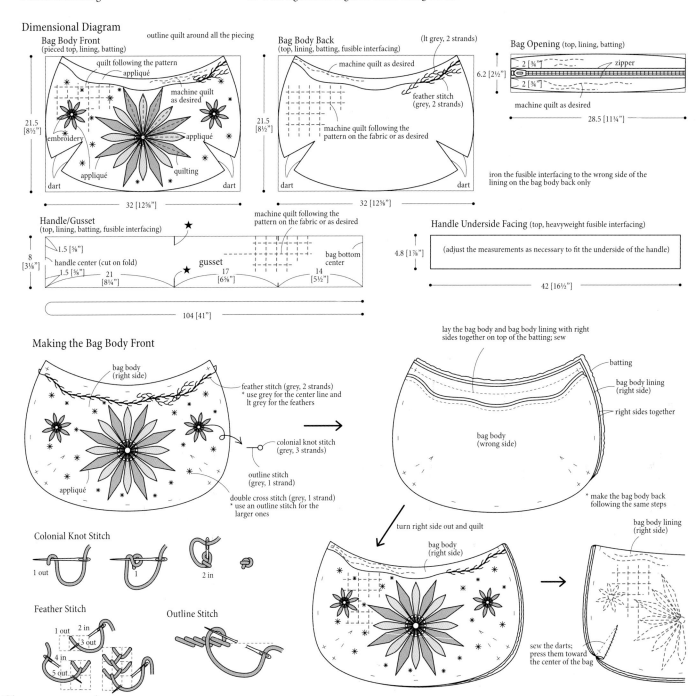

Dimensional Diagram

Making the Bag Body Front

Colonial Knot Stitch

Feather Stitch

Outline Stitch

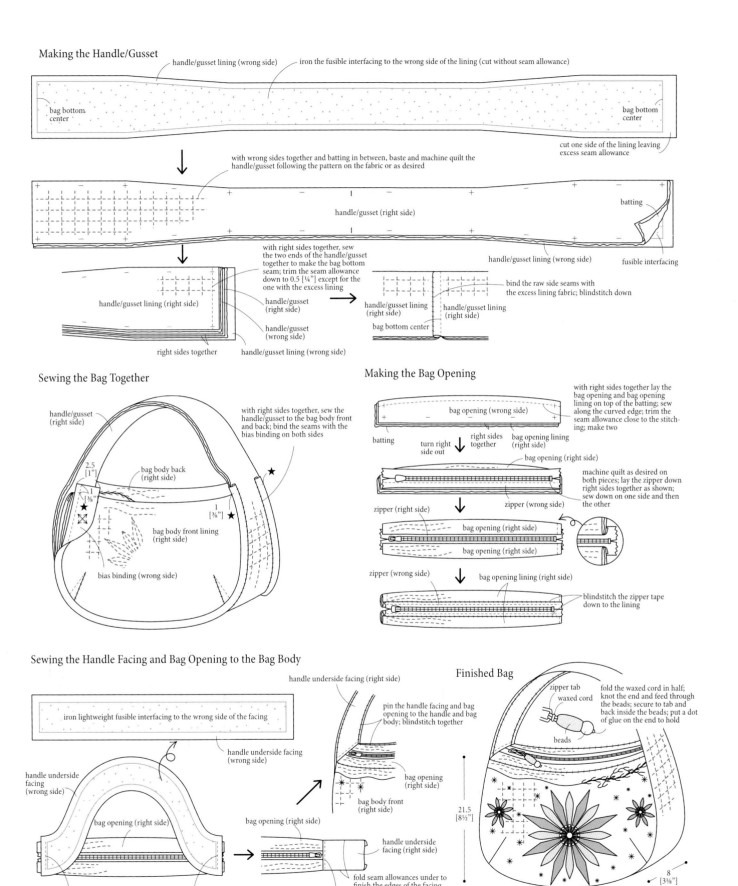

Making the Handle/Gusset

handle/gusset lining (wrong side)

iron the fusible interfacing to the wrong side of the lining (cut without seam allowance)

bag bottom center

bag bottom center

cut one side of the lining leaving excess seam allowance

with wrong sides together and batting in between, baste and machine quilt the handle/gusset following the pattern on the fabric or as desired

handle/gusset (right side)

batting

handle/gusset lining (wrong side)

fusible interfacing

with right sides together, sew the two ends of the handle/gusset together to make the bag bottom seam; trim the seam allowance down to 0.5 [¼"] except for the one with the excess lining

handle/gusset lining (right side)

handle/gusset (right side)

handle/gusset (wrong side)

bind the raw side seams with the excess lining fabric; blindstitch down

handle/gusset lining (right side)

handle/gusset lining (right side)

bag bottom center

right sides together

handle/gusset lining (wrong side)

Sewing the Bag Together

handle/gusset (right side)

with right sides together, sew the handle/gusset to the bag body front and back; bind the seams with the bias binding on both sides

2.5 [1"]

1 [⅜"]

1 [⅜"]

★

bag body back (right side)

★

bag body front lining (right side)

bias binding (wrong side)

Making the Bag Opening

with right sides together lay the bag opening and bag opening lining on top of the batting; sew along the curved edge; trim the seam allowance close to the stitching; make two

bag opening (wrong side)

batting

turn right side out

right sides together

bag opening lining (right side)

bag opening (right side)

machine quilt as desired on both pieces; lay the zipper down right sides together as shown; sew down on one side and then the other

zipper (right side)

zipper (wrong side)

bag opening (right side)

bag opening (right side)

zipper (wrong side)

bag opening lining (right side)

blindstitch the zipper tape down to the lining

Sewing the Handle Facing and Bag Opening to the Bag Body

iron lightweight fusible interfacing to the wrong side of the facing

handle underside facing (right side)

handle underside facing (wrong side)

handle underside facing (wrong side)

bag opening (right side)

pin the handle facing and bag opening to the handle and bag body; blindstitch together

bag opening (right side)

bag body front (right side)

bag opening (right side)

handle underside facing (right side)

fold seam allowances under to finish the edges of the facing

with right sides together, sew the handle underside facing to the bag opening

press the seam allowance toward the facing; fold the edges under; machine stitch to secure

Finished Bag

zipper tab

waxed cord

fold the waxed cord in half; knot the end and feed through the beads; secure to tab and back inside the beads; put a dot of glue on the end to hold

beads

21.5 [8½"]

8 [3⅛"]

32 [12⅝"]

Red Star Bag ·······› *p.08* (full-size template/pattern - Side A of the pattern sheet insert)

▶ Materials Needed
Assorted fat quarters or scraps (appliqué)
Homespun (bag body, handle, pocket lining)
 - 110×60 cm [43¼" × 23⅝"]
Homespun (pocket, tab, button cover)
 - 40×20 cm [15¾" × 7⅞"]
Cotton print (lining) and Batting (each)
 - 110×60 cm [43¼"×23⅝"]
Homespun (bias binding, bag opening/handle)
 - 3.5×180 cm [1⅜"×71"]
Homespun (tab facing)
 - 2.5×6 cm [1" × 2⅜"]
Heavyweight fusible interfacing
 - 55×7 cm [21⅝" × 2¾"]

Fusible interfacing
 - 40×40 cm [15¾" × 15¾"]
Embroidery floss - colors as desired
3 Buttons - 2.5 cm [1"]
1 Magnetic closure button - 2.3 cm [⅞"]

▶ Instructions
1. Using the diagram below and the pattern, piece, appliqué, and embroider the bag body front.
2. With wrong sides together and batting in between, baste together the three layers; quilt.
3. Sew the darts on the bag body front and back. With right sides together, sew the side seams;

bind the raw edges.
4. Bind the bag opening. Make the two pockets. Sew them in place on the sides of the bag body.
5. Make the handle. Sew both ends in place at the side seams on the bag opening.
6. Make the tab and the covered magnetic buttons. Sew to the bag opening to finish.

Dimensional Diagram

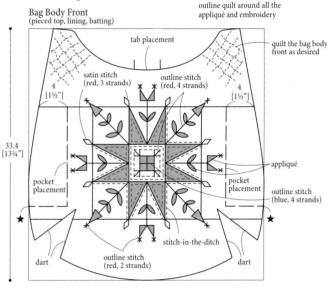

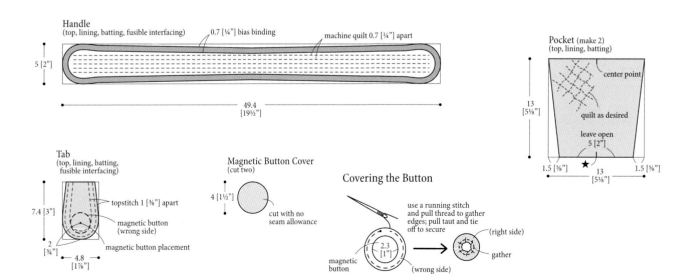

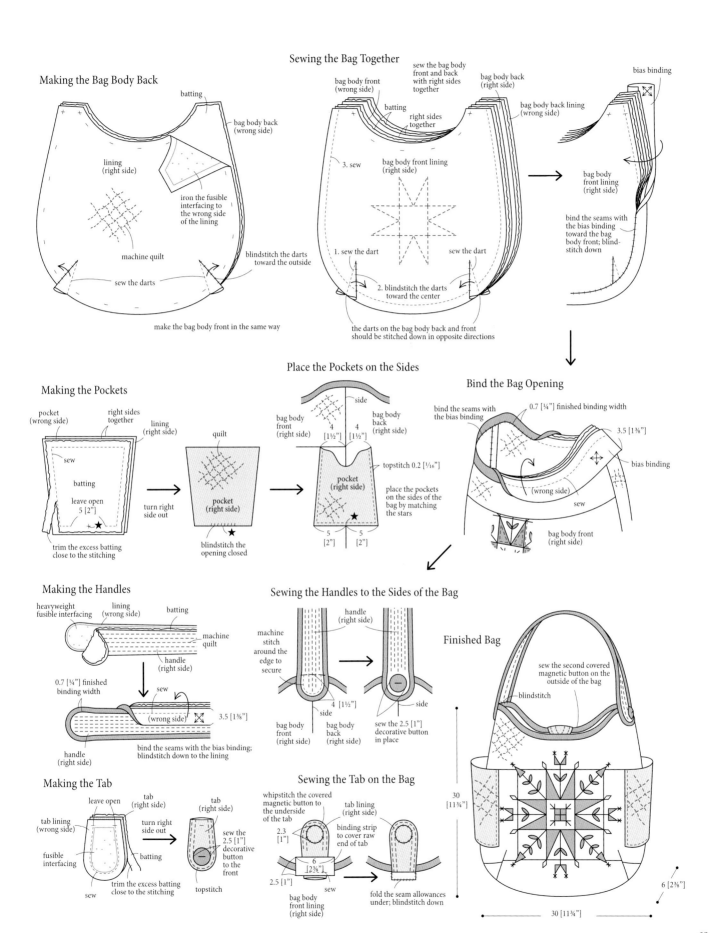

Making the Bag Body Back

batting

bag body back (wrong side)

lining (right side)

iron the fusible interfacing to the wrong side of the lining

machine quilt

blindstitch the darts toward the outside

sew the darts

make the bag body front in the same way

Sewing the Bag Together

sew the bag body front and back with right sides together

bag body front (wrong side)

bag body back (right side)

bias binding

batting

right sides together

bag body back lining (wrong side)

3. sew

bag body front lining (right side)

bag body front lining (right side)

bind the seams with the bias binding toward the bag body front; blindstitch down

1. sew the dart

sew the dart

2. blindstitch the darts toward the center

the darts on the bag body back and front should be stitched down in opposite directions

Making the Pockets

Place the Pockets on the Sides

pocket (wrong side)

right sides together

lining (right side)

sew

batting

leave open 5 [2"]

trim the excess batting close to the stitching

turn right side out

quilt

pocket (right side)

★

blindstitch the opening closed

side

bag body front (right side)

4 [1½"]

4 [1½"]

bag body back (right side)

topstitch 0.2 [1/16"]

pocket (right side)

place the pockets on the sides of the bag by matching the stars

5 [2"]

5 [2"]

Bind the Bag Opening

bind the seams with the bias binding

0.7 [¼"] finished binding width

3.5 [1⅜"]

bias binding

(wrong side)

sew

bag body front (right side)

Making the Handles

heavyweight fusible interfacing

lining (wrong side)

batting

machine quilt

handle (right side)

0.7 [¼"] finished binding width

sew

(wrong side)

3.5 [1⅜"]

handle (right side)

bind the seams with the bias binding; blindstitch down to the lining

Sewing the Handles to the Sides of the Bag

handle (right side)

machine stitch around the edge to secure

side

4 [1½"]

side

bag body front (right side)

bag body back (right side)

sew the 2.5 [1"] decorative button in place

Finished Bag

sew the second covered magnetic button on the outside of the bag

blindstitch

30 [11¾"]

30 [11¾"]

6 [2⅜"]

Making the Tab

leave open

tab (right side)

tab lining (wrong side)

turn right side out

tab (right side)

fusible interfacing

batting

sew

trim the excess batting close to the stitching

topstitch

sew the 2.5 [1"] decorative button to the front

Sewing the Tab on the Bag

whipstitch the covered magnetic button to the underside of the tab

2.3 [1"]

tab lining (right side)

binding strip to cover raw end of tab

6 [2⅜"]

2.5 [1"]

sew

bag body front lining (right side)

fold the seam allowances under; blindstitch down

3 Blue Star Bag

p.10 (full-size template/pattern - Side A of the pattern sheet insert)

▸ Materials Needed

Assorted fat quarters or scraps (appliqué, tab)
Homespun (bag body front, bag opening, gusset/ bottom) - 110 × 35 cm [43¼" × 13¾"]
Homespun (pocket, bag body back) - 60 × 35 cm [23⅝" × 13¾"]
Cotton print (lining) and Batting (each) - 110 × 55 cm [43¼" × 21⅝"]
Homespun (bias binding, pocket) - 3.5 × 25 cm [1⅜" × 9¾"]
Homespun (bias binding, seams) - 2.5 × 210 cm [1" × 82¾"]
Fusible interfacing - 100 × 40 cm [39⅜" × 15¾"]
1 Zipper - 30 cm [11¾"]
Leather handles - 1 pair
Embroidery floss - colors as desired
1 Bead - (zipper pull)
Waxed cord - (zipper pull) 0.3 × 10 cm [⅛" × 4"]

▸ Instructions

1. Using the diagram below and the pattern, with wrong sides together and batting in between, baste and quilt the bag body front and back.
2. Appliqué and embroider the pocket front. With wrong sides together, baste and quilt the pocket; bind the top pocket opening.
3. Lay the pocket on top of the bag body front; baste around the sides/bottom.
4. Make the bag opening and gusset/bottom and sew them together as shown.
5. With right sides together and zipper open, sew the bag body front, back, and bag opening/gusset/bottom together. Bind the raw edges.
6. Sew on the handles. Make and attach the zipper pull to finish.

Dimensional Diagram

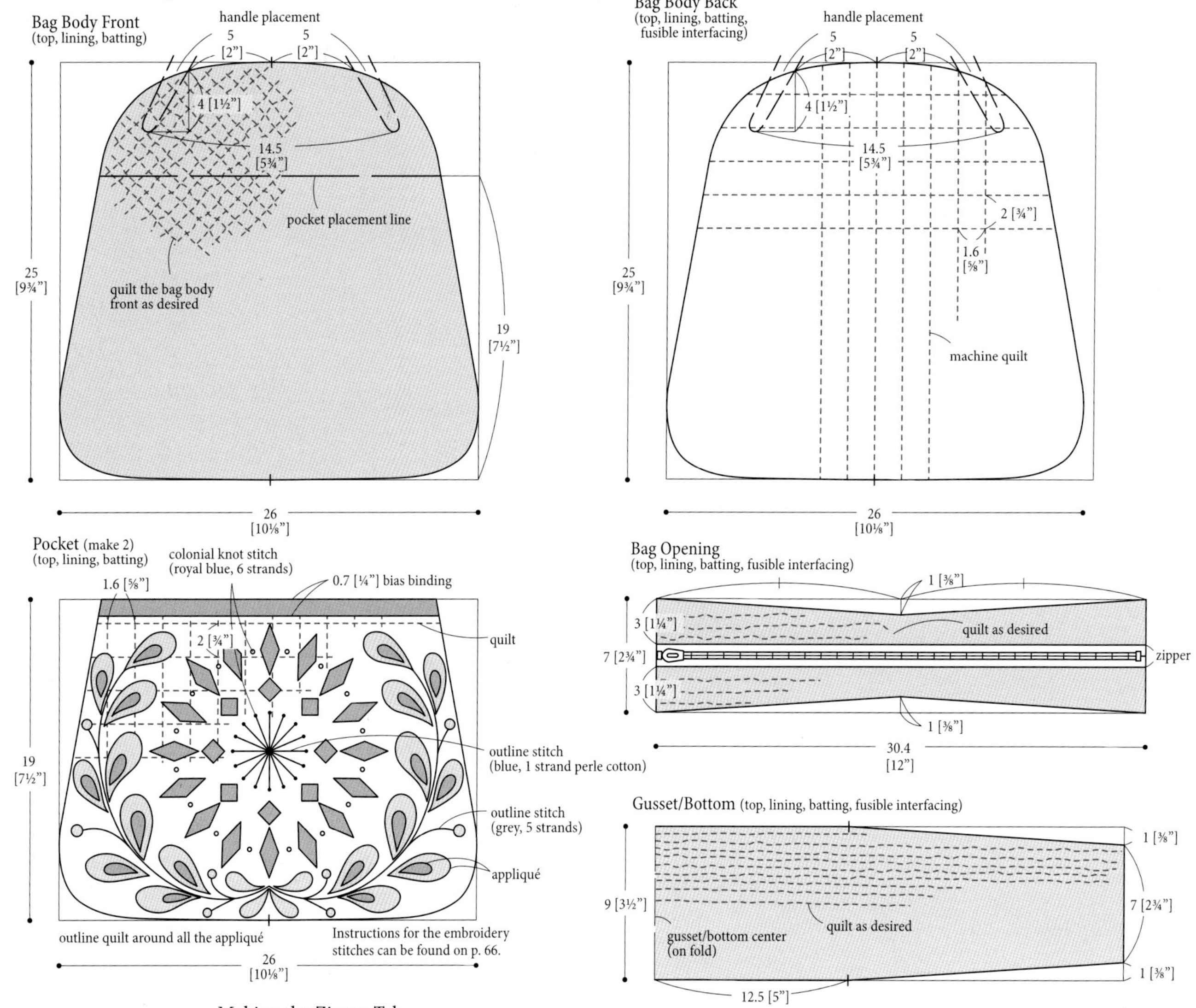
Bag Body Front
(top, lining, batting)
handle placement
5 [2"]
5 [2"]
4 [1½"]
14.5 [5¾"]
pocket placement line
quilt the bag body front as desired
25 [9¾"]
19 [7½"]
26 [10⅛"]
Bag Body Back
(top, lining, batting, fusible interfacing)
handle placement
5 [2"]
5 [2"]
4 [1½"]
14.5 [5¾"]
2 [¾"]
1.6 [⅝"]
machine quilt
25 [9¾"]
26 [10⅛"]
Pocket (make 2)
(top, lining, batting)
colonial knot stitch
(royal blue, 6 strands)
1.6 [⅝"]
0.7 [¼"] bias binding
2 [¾"]
quilt
19 [7½"]
outline stitch
(blue, 1 strand perle cotton)
outline stitch
(grey, 5 strands)
appliqué
outline quilt around all the appliqué
Instructions for the embroidery stitches can be found on p. 66.
26 [10⅛"]
Bag Opening
(top, lining, batting, fusible interfacing)
1 [⅜"]
3 [1¼"]
quilt as desired
7 [2¾"]
zipper
3 [1¼"]
1 [⅜"]
30.4 [12"]
Gusset/Bottom (top, lining, batting, fusible interfacing)
1 [⅜"]
9 [3½"]
7 [2¾"]
quilt as desired
gusset/bottom center (on fold)
1 [⅜"]
12.5 [5"]
58 [22⅞"]

Making the Zipper Tab

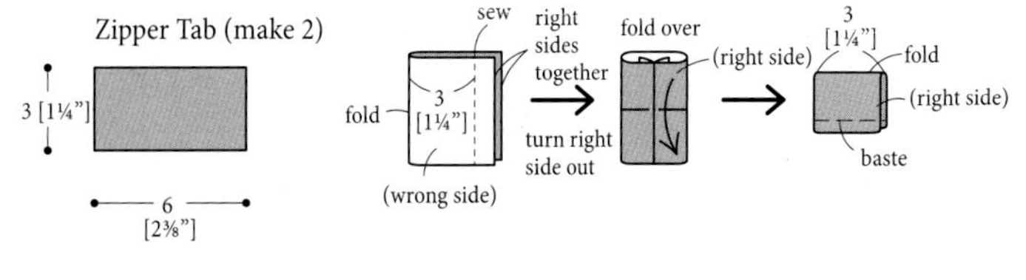
Zipper Tab (make 2)
3 [1¼"]
6 [2⅜"]
sew
right sides together
fold
3 [1¼"]
(wrong side)
turn right side out
fold over
(right side)
3 [1¼"]
fold
(right side)
baste

Making the Bag Front and Back

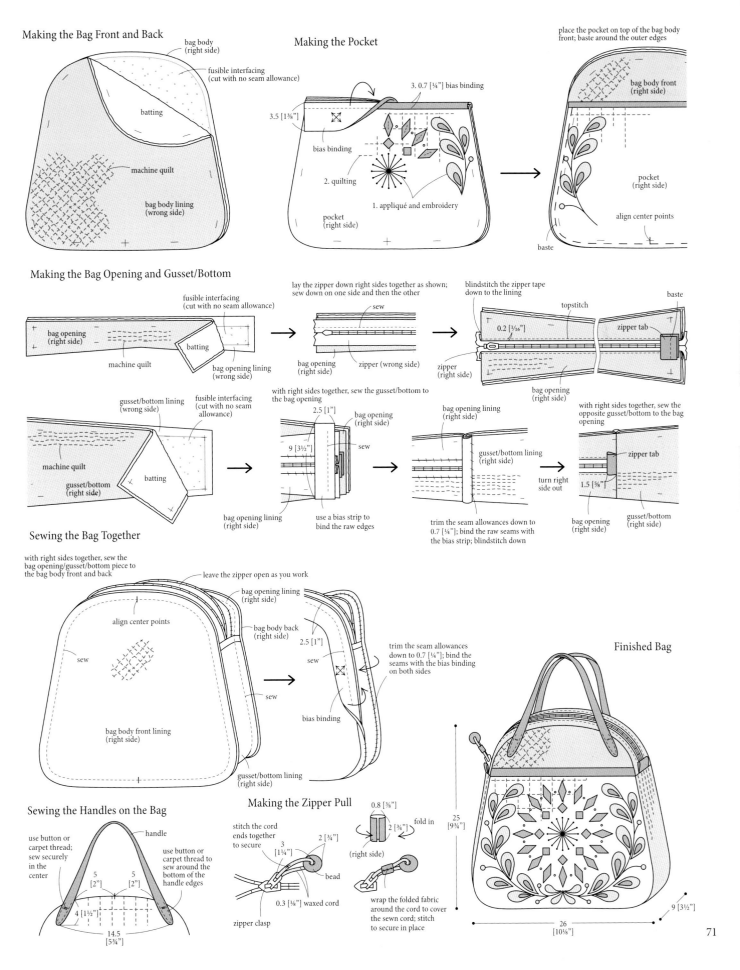

bag body (right side)

fusible interfacing (cut with no seam allowance)

batting

machine quilt

bag body lining (wrong side)

Making the Pocket

3. 0.7 [¼"] bias binding

3.5 [1⅜"]

bias binding

2. quilting

1. appliqué and embroidery

pocket (right side)

place the pocket on top of the bag body front; baste around the outer edges

bag body front (right side)

pocket (right side)

align center points

baste

Making the Bag Opening and Gusset/Bottom

fusible interfacing (cut with no seam allowance)

bag opening (right side)

machine quilt

bag opening lining (wrong side)

batting

lay the zipper down right sides together as shown; sew down on one side and then the other

sew

bag opening (right side)

zipper (wrong side)

blindstitch the zipper tape down to the lining

topstitch

baste

0.2 [¹⁄₁₆"]

zipper tab

zipper (right side)

bag opening (right side)

gusset/bottom lining (wrong side)

fusible interfacing (cut with no seam allowance)

machine quilt

gusset/bottom (right side)

batting

with right sides together, sew the gusset/bottom to the bag opening

2.5 [1"]

bag opening (right side)

9 [3½"]

sew

bag opening lining (right side)

use a bias strip to bind the raw edges

bag opening lining (right side)

gusset/bottom lining (right side)

trim the seam allowances down to 0.7 [¼"]; bind the raw seams with the bias strip; blindstitch down

with right sides together, sew the opposite gusset/bottom to the bag opening

zipper tab

turn right side out

1.5 [⅝"]

bag opening (right side)

gusset/bottom (right side)

Sewing the Bag Together

with right sides together, sew the bag opening/gusset/bottom piece to the bag body front and back

leave the zipper open as you work

bag opening lining (right side)

align center points

bag body back (right side)

sew

2.5 [1"]

sew

trim the seam allowances down to 0.7 [¼"]; bind the seams with the bias binding on both sides

sew

bias binding

bag body front lining (right side)

gusset/bottom lining (right side)

Finished Bag

25 [9¾"]

26 [10⅛"]

9 [3½"]

Sewing the Handles on the Bag

use button or carpet thread; sew securely in the center

handle

use button or carpet thread to sew around the bottom of the handle edges

5 [2"]

5 [2"]

4 [1½"]

14.5 [5¾"]

Making the Zipper Pull

stitch the cord ends together to secure

3 [1¼"]

2 [¾"]

bead

0.3 [⅛"] waxed cord

zipper clasp

0.8 [⅜"]

2 [¾"]

fold in

(right side)

wrap the folded fabric around the cord to cover the sewn cord; stitch to secure in place

4 Little Birds Shoulder Bag ······· *p.12*   (full-size template/pattern - Side A of the pattern sheet insert)

► Materials Needed
Assorted fat quarters or scraps (appliqué, bag body front A, shoulder strap, strap tab)
Homespun (bag body front B, bag body back, bag opening, gusset/bottom, pockets, flaps)
 – 110×60 cm [43¼" × 23⅝"]
Cotton print (lining, pocket facing)
 – 110×60 cm [43¼" × 23⅝"]
Batting
 – 90×60 cm [35⅜" × 23⅝"]
Homespun (bias binding, bag body front A/B)
 – 3.5×25 cm [1⅜"×9¾"]
Homespun (bias binding, seams)
 – 2.5×200 cm [1"×78¾"]
Fusible interfacing（bag opening）
 – 40×10 cm [15¾" × 4"]

Lightweight fusible interfacing (bag body back)
 – 30×30 cm [11¾" × 11¾"]
Heavyweight fusible interfacing (gusset/bottom)
 – 60×10 cm [23⅝" × 4"]
Double-sided fusible interfacing (facing)
 – 30×30 cm [11¾" × 11¾"]
1 Zipper (bag body front A/B) - 19 cm [7½"]
1 Zipper (bag opening) - 30 cm [11¾"]
Woven webbing (shoulder strap)
 – 4 ×150 cm [1½" ×59"]
1 Double-ring; 1 Rectangle ring hardware (shoulder strap) 4 cm [1½"] wide
2 Magnetic closure buttons - 2.3 cm [⅞"]
Embroidery floss - colors as desired
1 Bead - (zipper pull)
Waxed cord - (zipper pull) 0.3 × 20 cm [⅛" × 7⅞"]

► Instructions
1. Using the diagram below and the pattern, appliqué and embroider the pocket and flaps.
2. Follow the instructions for making each of the sections; sewing, quilting, and inserting the zippers and shoulder strap.
3. Make the front pocket facing; baste the front pocket facing to the bag body front after the zipper is sewn in.
4. With right sides together and zipper open, sew the bag body front, back, and bag opening/gusset/bottom together (the shoulder strap will be inside); bind seams.
4. Sew in covered magnetic buttons and attach zipper pull to finish.

Dimensional Diagram

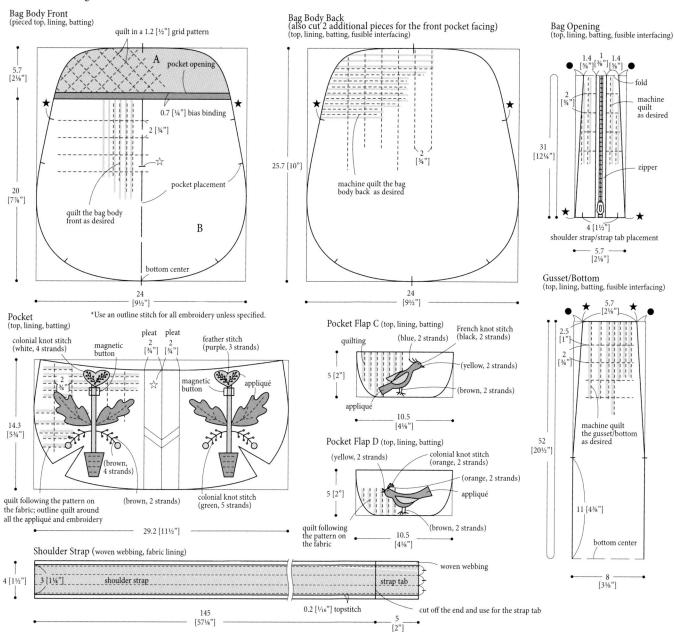

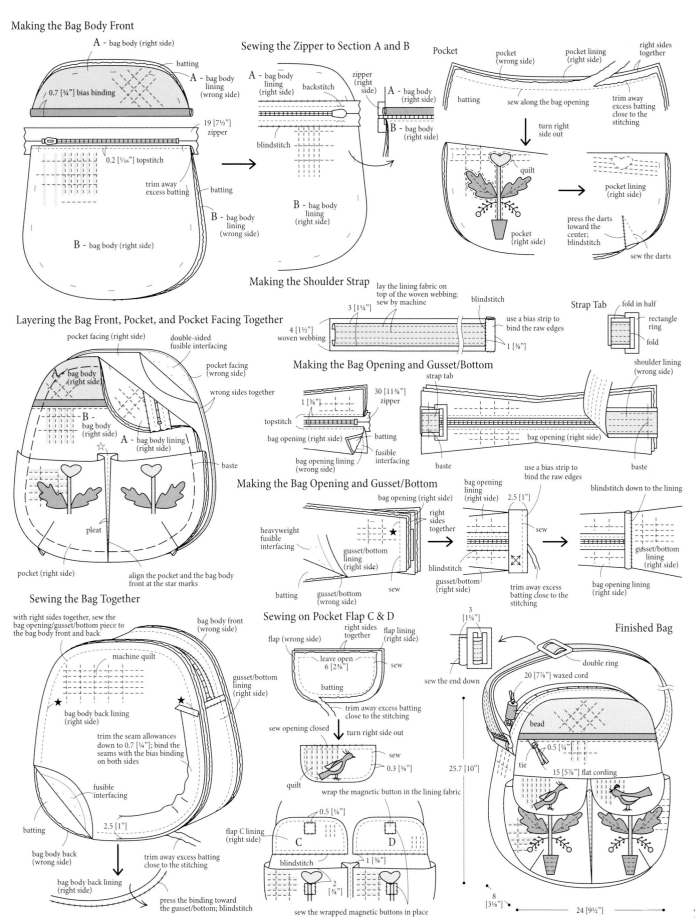

Making the Bag Body Front

A - bag body (right side)
batting
A - bag body lining (wrong side)
0.7 [¼"] bias binding
19 [7½"] zipper
0.2 [1/16"] topstitch
trim away excess batting
batting
B - bag body lining (wrong side)
B - bag body (right side)

Sewing the Zipper to Section A and B

A - bag body lining (right side)
backstitch
zipper (right side)
A - bag body (right side)
B - bag body (right side)
blindstitch
B - bag body lining (right side)

Pocket

pocket (wrong side)
pocket lining (right side)
right sides together
batting
sew along the bag opening
trim away excess batting close to the stitching
turn right side out
quilt
pocket (right side)
pocket lining (right side)
press the darts toward the center; blindstitch
sew the darts

Layering the Bag Front, Pocket, and Pocket Facing Together

pocket facing (right side)
double-sided fusible interfacing
pocket facing (wrong side)
wrong sides together
A - bag body (right side)
B - bag body (right side)
A - bag body lining (right side)
baste
pleat
pocket (right side)
align the pocket and the bag body front at the star marks

Making the Shoulder Strap

lay the lining fabric on top of the woven webbing; sew by machine
blindstitch
3 [1¼"]
4 [1½"] woven webbing
use a bias strip to bind the raw edges
1 [⅜"]

Strap Tab

fold in half
rectangle ring
fold
shoulder lining (wrong side)

Making the Bag Opening and Gusset/Bottom

30 [11¾"] zipper
strap tab
1 [⅜"]
topstitch
bag opening (right side)
bag opening lining (wrong side)
batting
fusible interfacing
use a bias strip to bind the raw edges
bag opening (right side)
baste
baste

Making the Bag Opening and Gusset/Bottom

bag opening (right side)
heavyweight fusible interfacing
gusset/bottom lining (right side)
right sides together
bag opening lining (right side)
2.5 [1"]
sew
blindstitch down to the lining
batting
gusset/bottom (wrong side)
sew
blindstitch
gusset/bottom (right side)
trim away excess batting close to the stitching
gusset/bottom lining (right side)
bag opening lining (right side)

Sewing the Bag Together

with right sides together, sew the bag opening/gusset/bottom piece to the bag body front and back
bag body front (wrong side)
machine quilt
gusset/bottom lining (right side)
bag body back lining (right side)
trim the seam allowances down to 0.7 [¼"]; bind the seams with the bias binding on both sides
fusible interfacing
batting
2.5 [1"]
bag body back (wrong side)
bag body back lining (right side)
trim away excess batting close to the stitching
press the binding toward the gusset/bottom; blindstitch

Sewing on Pocket Flap C & D

flap (wrong side)
right sides together
flap lining (right side)
leave open 6 [2⅜"]
sew
batting
trim away excess batting close to the stitching
sew opening closed
turn right side out
sew
0.3 [⅛"]
quilt
wrap the magnetic button in the lining fabric
0.5 [¼"]
flap C lining (right side)
C
D
blindstitch
1 [⅜"]
2 [¾"]
sew the wrapped magnetic buttons in place

Finished Bag

3 [1¼"]
sew the end down
double ring
20 [7⅞"] waxed cord
bead
0.5 [¼"]
tie
15 [5⅞"] flat cording
25.7 [10"]
8 [3⅛"]
24 [9½"]

73

5 Leaves Galore Granny Bag ······· *p.14* (full-size template/pattern - Side A of the pattern sheet insert)

▶ Materials Needed
Assorted fat quarters or scraps (appliqué, tab)
Cotton print (bag body)
  - 110×60 cm [43¼" × 23⅝"]
Homespun (gusset)
  - 30×25 cm [11¾" × 9¾"]
Cotton print (lining) and Batting (each)
  - 110×60 cm [43¼" × 23⅝"]
Homespun (bias binding, bag opening)
  - 3.5×80 cm [1⅜" × 31½"]
Homespun Piping (bias binding for piping
  between bag body sections)
  - 2.5×180 cm [1" ×71"] bias binding
  - 0.3×170 cm [⅛" ×67"] cord for inside piping
Cotton print (bias binding, seams)
  - 2.5×60 cm [1" × 23⅝"]
Cotton woven webbing (handles)

  - 3 ×190 cm [1¼" ×75"]
1 Magnetic closure button - 2 cm [¾"]
Fusible interfacing (bag opening)
  - 70×30 cm [27½" × 11¾"]
Heavyweight fusible interfacing (gusset/bottom)
  - 30×20 cm [11¾" × 7⅞"]
Embroidery floss - colors as desired

▶ Instructions
1. Using the diagram below and the pattern, appliqué and embroider the four bag body front sections.
2. With wrong sides together and batting in between, baste and quilt each section.
3. With right sides together, sew sections A¹, A², C and D together with the piping in between. Make the bag body back in the same way.

4. With right sides together, sew the bag body front and back together along the bottom. Bind the seams. Bind the bag opening.
5. Make the gussets; bind the top. With wrong sides together, sew the gussets to the bag body.
6. Fold the cotton woven webbing in half and use it to bind the gusset seams and to create the handles. Pin in place; topstitch close to the edges all the way around.
7. Make the button tabs with the magnetic buttons in between. Sew them in place on either side of the bag opening to finish.

Dimensional Diagram

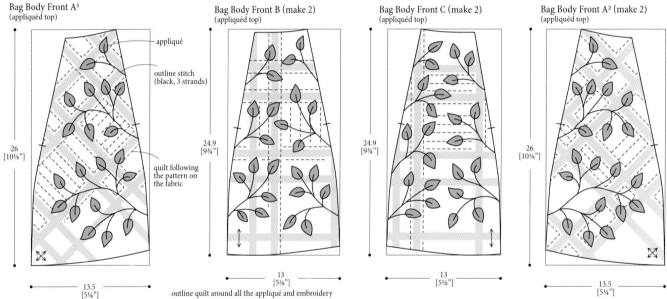

Bag Body Front A¹
(appliquéd top)

— appliqué

outline stitch
(black, 3 strands)

quilt following
the pattern on
the fabric

26
[10⅛"]

13.5
[5¼"]

Bag Body Front B (make 2)
(appliquéd top)

24.9
[9¾"]

13
[5⅛"]

outline quilt around all the appliqué and embroidery

Bag Body Front C (make 2)
(appliquéd top)

24.9
[9¾"]

13
[5⅛"]

Bag Body Back
(lining, batting, fusible interfacing); cut each lining piece in reverse with no appliqué

Bag Body Front A² (make 2)
(appliquéd top)

26
[10⅛"]

13.5
[5¼"]

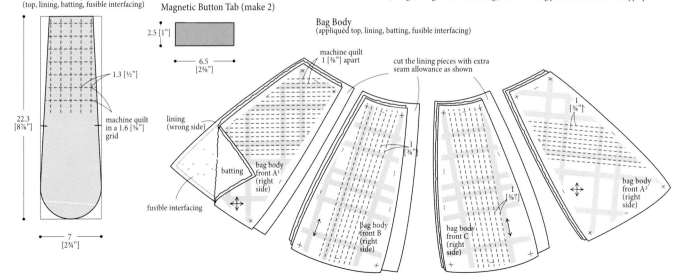

Gusset (make 2)
(top, lining, batting, fusible interfacing)

Magnetic Button Tab (make 2)

2.5 [1"]

6.5
[2⅝"]

1.3 [½"]

22.3
[8⅞"]

machine quilt
in a 1.6 [⅝"]
grid

7
[2¾"]

Bag Body
(appliquéd top, lining, batting, fusible interfacing)

machine quilt
1 [⅜"] apart

cut the lining pieces with extra
seam allowance as shown

lining
(wrong side)

batting

fusible interfacing

bag body
front A¹
(right
side)

bag body
front B
(right
side)

bag body
front C
(right
side)

1
[⅜"]

1
[⅜"]

1
[⅜"]

bag body
front A²
(right
side)

74

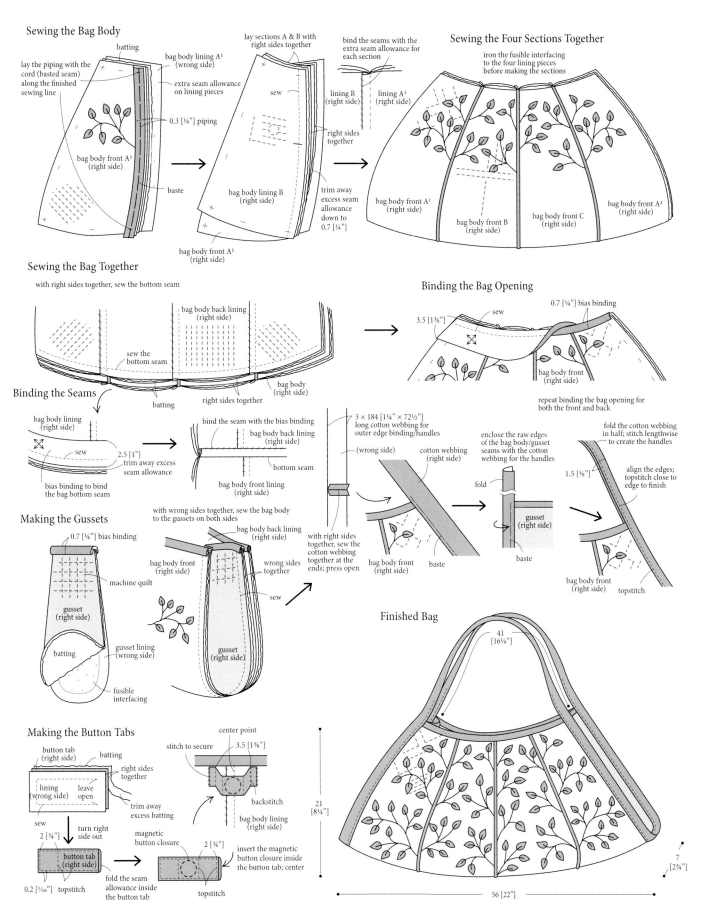

Sewing the Bag Body

batting

lay the piping with the cord (basted seam) along the finished sewing line

bag body lining A¹ (wrong side)

extra seam allowance on lining pieces

0.3 [⅛"] piping

bag body front A¹ (right side)

baste

lay sections A & B with right sides together

sew

bag body lining B (right side)

right sides together

bag body front A¹ (right side)

trim away excess seam allowance down to 0.7 [¼"]

bind the seams with the extra seam allowance for each section

lining B (right side)

lining A¹ (right side)

Sewing the Four Sections Together

iron the fusible interfacing to the four lining pieces before making the sections

bag body front A¹ (right side)

bag body front B (right side)

bag body front C (right side)

bag body front A² (right side)

Sewing the Bag Together

with right sides together, sew the bottom seam

bag body back lining (right side)

sew the bottom seam

right sides together

batting

bag body (right side)

Binding the Bag Opening

3.5 [1⅜"]

sew

0.7 [¼"] bias binding

bag body front (right side)

repeat binding the bag opening for both the front and back

Binding the Seams

bag body lining (right side)

sew

2.5 [1"] trim away excess seam allowance

bias binding to bind the bag bottom seam

bind the seam with the bias binding

bag body back lining (right side)

bottom seam

bag body front lining (right side)

3 × 184 [1¼" × 72½"] long cotton webbing for outer edge binding/handles

(wrong side)

cotton webbing (right side)

with right sides together, sew the cotton webbing together at the ends; press open

bag body front (right side)

baste

enclose the raw edges of the bag body/gusset seams with the cotton webbing for the handles

fold

gusset (right side)

baste

fold the cotton webbing in half; stitch lengthwise to create the handles

1.5 [⅝"]

align the edges; topstitch close to edge to finish

bag body front (right side)

topstitch

Making the Gussets

0.7 [¼"] bias binding

machine quilt

gusset (right side)

batting

gusset lining (wrong side)

fusible interfacing

with wrong sides together, sew the bag body to the gussets on both sides

bag body back lining (right side)

bag body front (right side)

wrong sides together

sew

gusset (right side)

Finished Bag

41 [16⅛"]

21 [8¼"]

7 [2¾"]

56 [22"]

Making the Button Tabs

button tab (right side)

batting

right sides together

lining (wrong side)

leave open

trim away excess batting

sew

2 [¾"]

turn right side out

button tab (right side)

0.2 [1/16"] topstitch

fold the seam allowance inside the button tab

center point

stitch to secure

3.5 [1⅜"]

backstitch

bag body lining (right side)

magnetic button closure

2 [¾"]

insert the magnetic button closure inside the button tab; center

topstitch

Wildflower Handbag ------- p.16 (full-size template/pattern - Side A of the pattern sheet insert)

▶ Materials Needed
Assorted fat quarters or scraps (appliqué, tab)
Homespun (pockets, gusset/bottom, zipper pull)
 - 110×20 cm [43¼" × 7⅞"]
Homespun (appliquéd "soil" all four sides)
 - 110×20 cm [43¼" × 7⅞"]
Homespun (bag body)
 - 80×20 cm [31½" × 7⅞"]
Homespun (handles)
 - 40×15 cm [15¾" × 5⅞"]
Cotton print (lining) and Batting (each)
 - 80×55 cm [31½" × 21⅝"]
Homespun (bias binding)
 - 3.5×35 cm [1⅜" × 13¾"] (2 for pockets)
 - 3.5×70 cm [1⅜" × 27½"] (bag opening)

 - 3.8×130 cm [1¾" ×51¼"] (bag body seams)
1 Zipper (pocket) - 30 cm [11¾"]
1 Zipper (bag opening) - 33 cm [13"]
Woven webbing (inside handles)
 - 2 ×80 cm [¾"×31½"]
Lightweight fusible interfacing（pockets)
 - 40×40 cm [15¾" × 15¾"]
Heavyweight fusible interfacing (gusset/bottom)
 - 15×55 cm [5⅞" × 21⅝"]
2 Magnetic closure buttons - 2 cm [¾"]
2 Wooden beads (zipper pull)
Embroidery floss - colors as desired

▶ Instructions
1. Using the diagram below and the pattern, ap-

pliqué and embroider the front and back pockets.
2. Cut out the two bag body pieces. With wrong sides together and batting in between, baste and quilt the bag body front and back and the pockets. Bind the top edges of all.
3. Baste the front pocket to the bag body front.
4. Sew in the zipper along with the back pocket to the bag body back.
5. Sew in the opening zipper. Make the handles; sew them in place on either side of the bag opening zipper.
6. Make the gusset/bottom. With wrong sides together, sew the bag body to the gusset/bottom.
7. Bind the seams. Make and attach the zipper pull to finish.

Dimensional Diagram

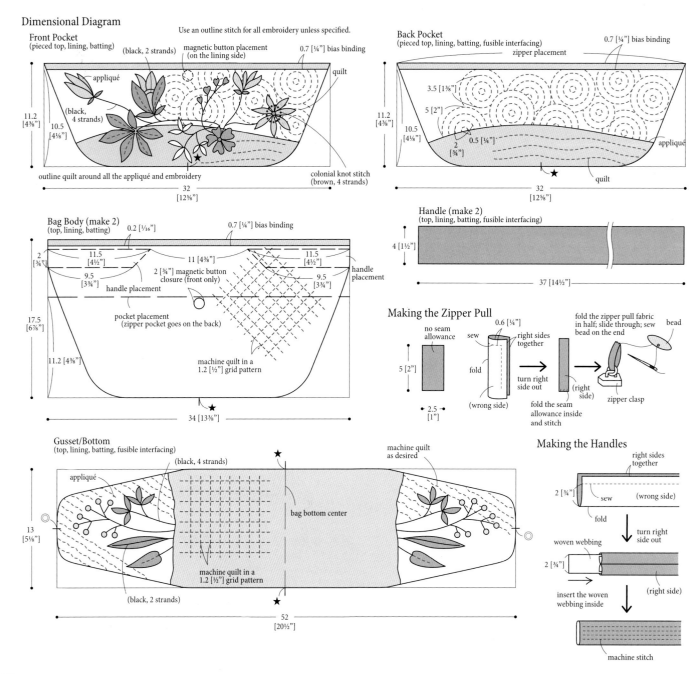

Making the Pockets

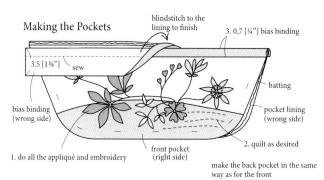

blindstitch to the lining to finish

3. 0.7 [¼"] bias binding

3.5 [1⅜"] sew

bias binding (wrong side)

batting

pocket lining (wrong side)

2. quilt as desired

1. do all the appliqué and embroidery

front pocket (right side)

make the back pocket in the same way as for the front

Making the Bag Body

blindstitch to the lining to finish

0.7 [¼"] bias binding

3.5 [1⅜"] sew

bias binding (wrong side)

bag body (right side)

machine quilt

batting

bag body lining (wrong side)

fusible interfacing

make two of the bag body

Attaching the Pockets to the Bag Body

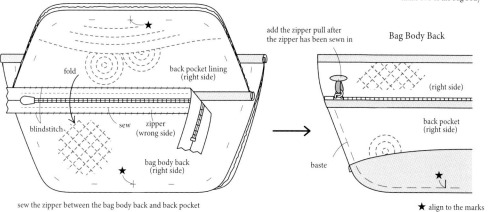

add the zipper pull after the zipper has been sewn in

fold

back pocket lining (right side)

blindstitch

sew

zipper (wrong side)

bag body back (right side)

sew the zipper between the bag body back and back pocket

Bag Body Back

(right side)

back pocket (right side)

baste

★ align to the marks

Bag Body Front

(right side)

front pocket (right side)

baste

★ align to the marks

sew the magnetic buttons between the bag body front and the front pocket; directions on p. 88

Sewing in the Zipper

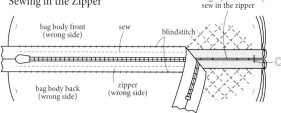

align so that the binding edges just touch as you sew in the zipper

bag body front (wrong side)

sew

blindstitch

bag body back (wrong side)

zipper (wrong side)

Sewing on the Handles

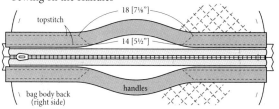

topstitch

18 [7⅛"]

14 [5½"]

handles

bag body back (right side)

Making the Gusset/Bottom

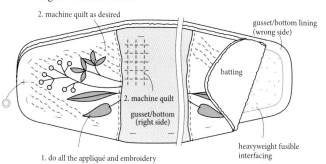

2. machine quilt as desired

gusset/bottom lining (wrong side)

batting

2. machine quilt

gusset/bottom (right side)

heavyweight fusible interfacing

1. do all the appliqué and embroidery

Sewing the Bag Together

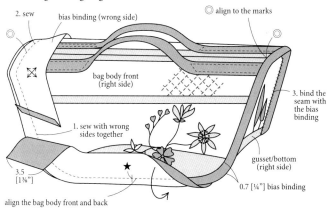

2. sew

bias binding (wrong side)

◎ align to the marks

bag body front (right side)

3. bind the seam with the bias binding

1. sew with wrong sides together

gusset/bottom (right side)

3.5 [1⅜"]

0.7 [¼"] bias binding

align the bag body front and back and gusset/bottom at the marks

Finished Bag

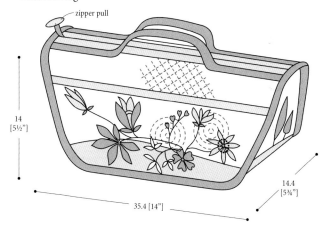

zipper pull

14 [5½"]

35.4 [14"]

14.4 [5¾"]

7 Soup Cup Pouch
p.18 (full-size template/pattern - Side A of the pattern sheet insert)

▶ **Materials Needed**
Assorted fat quarters or scraps (appliqué, bottom, handles, pouch opening)
Homespun (pouch background solid)
 - 30×25 cm [11¾" × 9¾"]
Homespun (lining) and Batting (each)
 - 40×30 cm [15¾" × 11¾"]
1 Zipper - 45 cm [17¾"]
Fusible interfacing (handle, bottom)
 - 8×20 cm [3⅛" × 7⅞"]

▶ **Instructions**
1. Using the diagram below and the pattern, appliqué the background fabric for the pouch body front and back. With right sides together, sew them at the side seam.
2. With wrong sides together, lay the appliquéd pouch body and lining on top of the batting; sew the top and bottom seams. Turn right side out and quilt.
3. Cut off the zipper stop end of the zipper and separate the teeth. Take the zipper slide clasp off and set aside for later. Pin the zipper, right sides together, along the top of the pouch; sew. Folding the zipper tape ends out of the way, fold the pouch in half with right sides together and sew the side seam. Trim away the excess seam allowance except for one side of the lining. Use the lining to bind the raw edge.
4. Put the zipper slide clasp back onto the aligned zipper teeth. Make and sew the zipper tab onto the end of the zipper tape to create a stop.
5. Make the pouch bottom; blindstitch to the bottom of the pouch.
6. Cut out two sets of handles (one in reverse). Iron fusible interfacing onto the wrong side; fold seam allowances under. With wrong sides together, align edges; topstitch all the way around. Blindstitch the handles to either side of the pouch to finish.

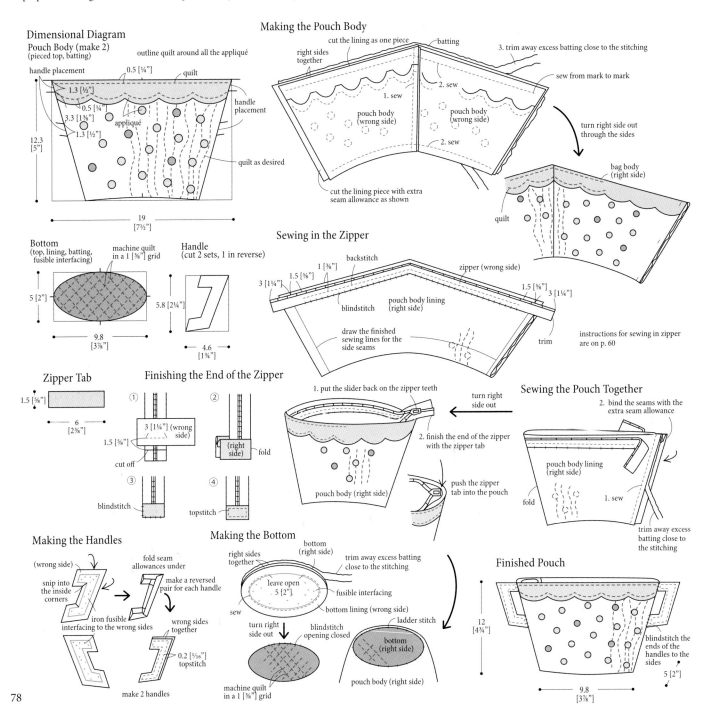

78

25 Hexagon Pincushion ⌐-----⌐ *p.38* (full-size template/pattern - Side A of the pattern sheet insert)

► Materials Needed
Assorted fat quarters or scraps (pincushion)
Clear template plastic (pouch background solid)
  – 10×10 cm [4” × 4”]
3 Beads
Candlewicking thread – grey (embroidery)
Fusible interfacing (bottom)
  – 10×20 cm [4” × 7⅞”]

► Instructions
1. Using the diagram below and the pattern, cut out the necessary pieces of fabric for each section.
2. With right sides together, sew the top of the pincushion together. Make the top base lining. Matching the edges with right sides together, pin the pincushion top and base lining to each other. Sew together leaving an opening for turning. Turn right side out and stuff with polyester filling. Sew opening closed.
3. Thread a needle with a fairly long piece of thread. Take the needle and come out of the top of the pincushion top; add beads; take needle back down through the top to the center bottom of the base where you started; pull the thread taut to create a tufted pincushion top.
4. Make the six sides of the pincushion. embroider along the pieced seams; insert the clear template plastic pieces. Make the bottom. Align the open edges of the sides with the side edges of the bottom. Sew each side in place. Stand up the sides and sew them together with a ladder stitch.
5. Place the pincushion down inside the box to finish.

Dimensional Diagram

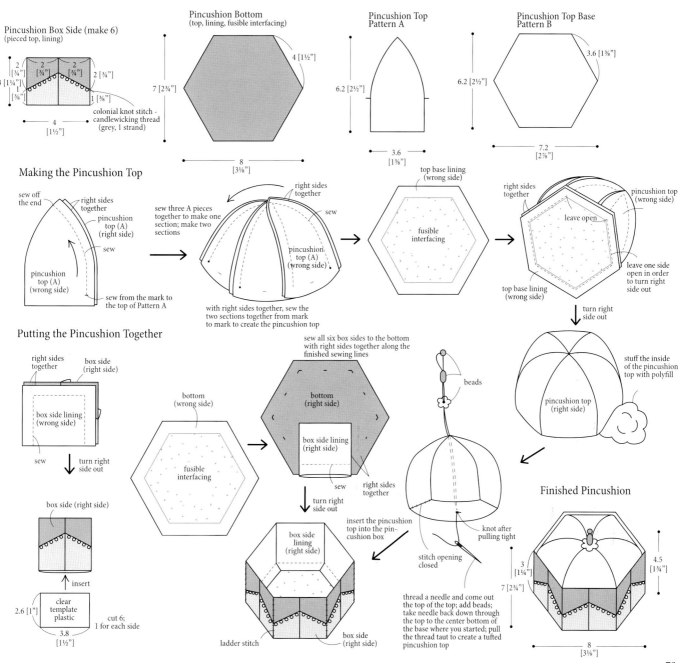

79

9 Owl Bag

$\cdots\cdots$ *p.20* (full-size template/pattern - Side A of the pattern sheet insert)

▶ Materials Needed
Assorted fat quarters or scraps (appliqué)
Cotton print (bag body front, back)
 - 60×30 cm [23⅝" × 11¾"]
Cotton print (bag sides, inner pocket lining)
 - 50×35 cm [19¾" × 13¾"]
Cotton print (pockets)
 - 40×25 cm [15¾" × 9¾"]
Homespun (bottom)
 - 30×20 cm [11¾" × 7⅞"]
Muslin (bottom facing)
 - 30×20 cm [11¾" × 7⅞"]
Homespun (lining)
 - 110×70 cm [43¼" × 27½"]
Batting
 - 110×60 cm [43¼" × 23⅝"]
Homespun (bias binding)

 - 3.5×35 cm [1⅜" × 13¾"] (side pockets)
 - 3.5×120 cm [1⅜" × 47¼"] (bag opening, inner pocket)
Cotton woven webbing (handles)
 - 2.5×170 cm [1" ×67"]
Heavyweight fusible interfacing (bottom)
 - 30×30 cm [11¾" × 11¾"]
Double-sided fusible interfacing (inner pockets)
 - 40×30 cm [15¾" × 11¾"]
Embroidery floss - colors as desired

▶ Instructions
1. Using the diagram below and the pattern, appliqué and embroider the front and back.
2. With wrong sides together and batting in between, baste and quilt the front and back.
3. Make the bag sides, outer pockets, and inner

pockets in the same way. Bind each top area after the quilting is complete.
4. Place the front and back on top of the inner pockets; baste along the side seams. Place the outer pockets on top of the sides; baste in place.
5. With wrong sides together, sew the front and back to the sides; press the seams toward the sides.
6. Cut the woven webbing in half. Cover the side seam with the webbing up one side and down the other to create the handles. Topstitch as shown.
7. With right sides together, sew the quilted bottom lining/facing to the bag body. Place the bag bottom over the quilted bottom (facing showing); blindstitch down to finish.

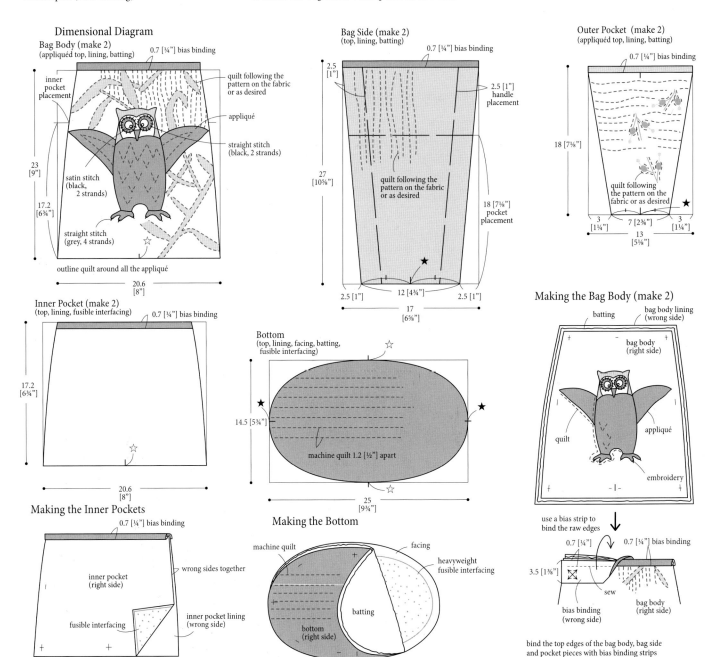

80

Sewing the Inner Pocket to the Bag Body

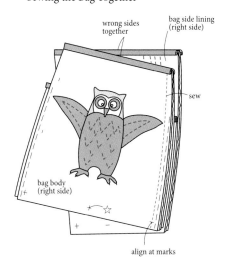

baste

wrong sides together

inner pocket lining (right side)

bag body (right side)

align at marks

☆

Sewing the Outer Pocket to the Bag Side

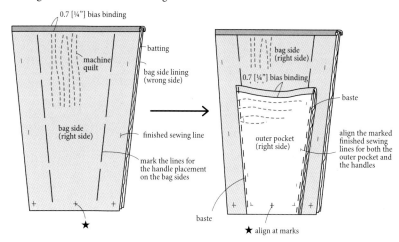

0.7 [¼"] bias binding

machine quilt

bag side (right side)

batting

bag side lining (wrong side)

finished sewing line

mark the lines for the handle placement on the bag sides

★

bag side (right side)

0.7 [¼"] bias binding

outer pocket (right side)

baste

align the marked finished sewing lines for both the outer pocket and the handles

baste

★ align at marks

Sewing the Bag Together

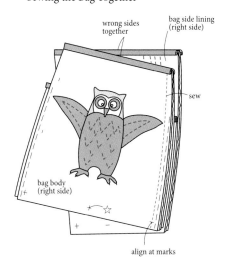

wrong sides together

bag side lining (right side)

sew

bag body (right side)

align at marks

☆

Adding the Handles to the Bag

press the seam allowances toward the side pockets

bag side lining (right side)

bag side (right side)

outer pocket (right side)

bag body (right side)

bag body (right side)

★

pin the cotton webbing for the handles in place, covering the seams; stitch as shown with a 0.2 [1/16"] topstitch

27 [10⅝"]

2.5 × 84 [1" × 33"] long cotton webbing for handles (cut 2)

0.2 [1/16"]

0.2 [1/16"] topstitch

bag body (right side)

☆

sew the handles to the bag on both sides in the same way

Sewing the Bottom to the Bag

With wrong sides together and batting in between, quilt the bottom lining and bottom facing together. Place this at the bottom opening of the bag body with right sides together; sew around the bottom; press the seam allowances toward the bottom; iron fusible interfacing to the wrong side of the bottom; turn the seam allowances under; blindstitch in place

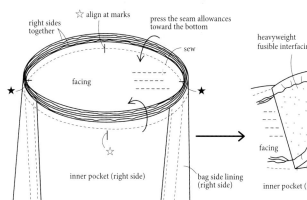

right sides together

☆ align at marks

press the seam allowances toward the bottom

sew

facing

inner pocket (right side)

bag side lining (right side)

★

★

☆

heavyweight fusible interfacing

fold seam allowances under

bottom lining (right side)

blindstitch

facing

inner pocket (right side)

bag side lining (right side)

Finished Bag

27 [10⅝"]

25 [9¾"]

14.5 [5¾"]

81

10 Flower & Basket Tote .... *p.24* (full-size template/pattern - Side A of the pattern sheet insert)

► Materials Needed
Assorted fat quarters or scraps (appliqué)
Cotton print (bag body front, back)
- 80×50 cm [31½" × 19¾"]
Homespun (gusset)
- 80×25 cm [31½" × 9¾"]
Cotton print (handles, basketweave bias strips)
- 110×35 cm [43¼" × 13¾"]
Cotton print (lining)
- 110×50 cm [43¼" × 19¾"]
Batting
- 110×40 cm [43¼" × 15¾"]
Cotton print (bias binding)
- 3.5×70 cm [1⅜" × 27½"] (bag opening)
- 2.5×140 cm [1" × 55⅛"] (seams)
- 2.5×30 cm [1" × 11¾"] (handle facing)

Homespun Piping (bias binding for piping between front and gussets)
- 2.5×140 cm [1" × 55⅛"] bias binding/piping
- 0.2×140 cm [¹⁄₁₆" × 55⅛"] cord for inside piping
Lightweight fusible interfacing (handle)
- 40×55 cm [15¾" × 21⅝"]
Embroidery floss - colors as desired

► Instructions
1. Using the diagram below and the pattern, appliqué and embroider the front. Make and appliqué the basketweave gussets.
2. With wrong sides together and batting in between, baste and quilt the bag front, back, and

gussets. Cut the bottom edge of the bag body back lining with extra seam allowance to use for binding bag bottom.
3. Make the piping (bias binding with cord inside); pin to the gussets; baste in place.
4. With right sides together, sew the front and back together. Use the excess lining to bind the bottom seam.
5. With right sides together, sew the gussets to the bag body. Bind the seams with the bias binding.
6. Bind the bag opening.
7. Make the handle. Sew to the inside bag opening. Use the handle facing bias strips to cover the seams; blindstitch down to finish.

Dimensional Diagram

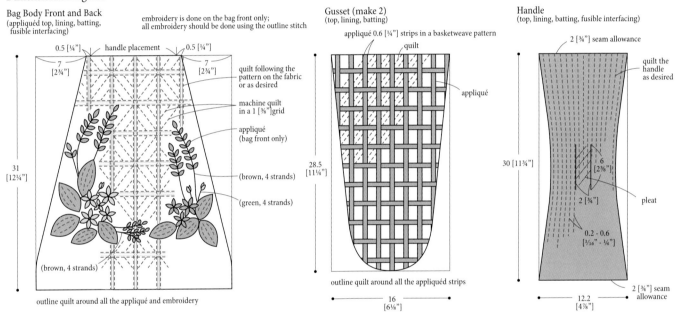

Bag Body Front and Back
(appliquéd top, lining, batting, fusible interfacing)

embroidery is done on the bag front only; all embroidery should be done using the outline stitch

0.5 [¼"]   handle placement   0.5 [¼"]
7 [2¾"]   7 [2¾"]

quilt following the pattern on the fabric or as desired

machine quilt in a 1 [⅜"]grid

appliqué (bag front only)

(brown, 4 strands)

(green, 4 strands)

31 [12¼"]

(brown, 4 strands)

outline quilt around all the appliqué and embroidery

27 [10⅝"]

Gusset (make 2)
(top, lining, batting)

appliqué 0.6 [¼"] strips in a basketweave pattern
quilt

appliqué

28.5 [11¼"]

outline quilt around all the appliquéd strips

16 [6⅛"]

Handle
(top, lining, batting, fusible interfacing)

2 [¾"] seam allowance

quilt the handle as desired

30 [11¾"]

6 [2⅜"]
2 [¾"]
pleat
0.2 - 0.6 [¹⁄₁₆" - ¼"]

2 [¾"] seam allowance

12.2 [4⅞"]

Appliquéing the Fabric Strips to the Gussets

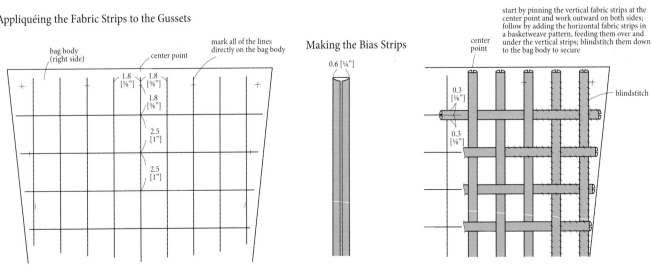

bag body (right side)

center point

mark all of the lines directly on the bag body

1.8 [⅝"]   1.8 [⅝"]
1.8 [⅝"]
2.5 [1"]
2.5 [1"]

Making the Bias Strips

0.6 [¼"]

center point

start by pinning the vertical fabric strips at the center point and work outward on both sides; follow by adding the horizontal fabric strips in a basketweave pattern, feeding them over and under the vertical strips; blindstitch them down to the bag body to secure

0.3 [⅛"]
0.3 [⅛"]

blindstitch

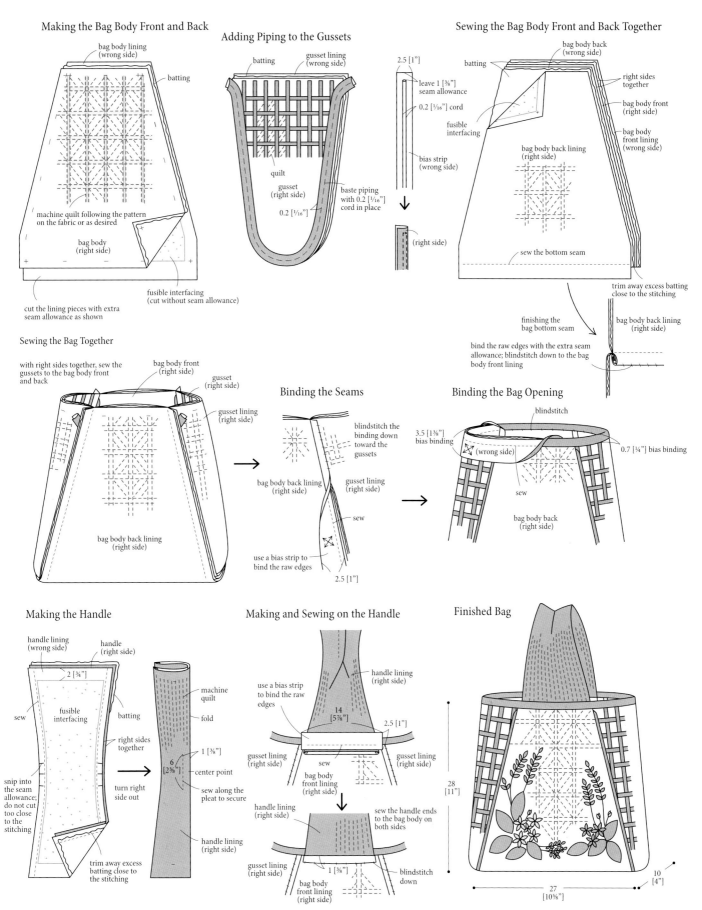

Making the Bag Body Front and Back

bag body lining (wrong side)

batting

machine quilt following the pattern on the fabric or as desired

bag body (right side)

cut the lining pieces with extra seam allowance as shown

fusible interfacing (cut without seam allowance)

Adding Piping to the Gussets

batting

gusset lining (wrong side)

quilt

gusset (right side)

0.2 [1/16"]

baste piping with 0.2 [1/16"] cord in place

2.5 [1"]

leave 1 [3/8"] seam allowance

0.2 [1/16"] cord

fusible interfacing

bias strip (wrong side)

(right side)

Sewing the Bag Body Front and Back Together

bag body back (wrong side)

batting

right sides together

bag body front (right side)

bag body front lining (wrong side)

bag body back lining (right side)

sew the bottom seam

trim away excess batting close to the stitching

finishing the bag bottom seam

bind the raw edges with the extra seam allowance; blindstitch down to the bag body front lining

bag body back lining (right side)

Sewing the Bag Together

with right sides together, sew the gussets to the bag body front and back

bag body front (right side)

gusset (right side)

gusset lining (right side)

bag body back lining (right side)

Binding the Seams

blindstitch the binding down toward the gussets

bag body back lining (right side)

gusset lining (right side)

sew

use a bias strip to bind the raw edges

2.5 [1"]

Binding the Bag Opening

blindstitch

3.5 [1 3/8"] bias binding

(wrong side)

sew

0.7 [1/4"] bias binding

bag body back (right side)

Making the Handle

handle lining (wrong side)

handle (right side)

2 [3/4"]

sew

fusible interfacing

batting

right sides together

snip into the seam allowance; do not cut too close to the stitching

trim away excess batting close to the stitching

turn right side out

machine quilt

fold

6 [2 3/8"]

1 [3/8"]

center point

sew along the pleat to secure

handle lining (right side)

Making and Sewing on the Handle

use a bias strip to bind the raw edges

handle lining (right side)

14 [5 7/8"]

2.5 [1"]

gusset lining (right side)

sew

gusset lining (right side)

bag body front lining (right side)

handle lining (right side)

gusset lining (right side)

bag body front lining (right side)

1 [3/8"]

sew the handle ends to the bag body on both sides

blindstitch down

Finished Bag

28 [11"]

27 [10 5/8"]

10 [4"]

11 Mini Flower Pouch ------- p.24

▶ Materials Needed
Assorted fat quarters or scraps (pouch body,
  appliqué, gussets, tab)
Cotton print (lining) and Batting (each)
  - 30×30 cm [11¾" × 11¾"]
Homespun (bias binding, around gusset)
  - 3.5×60 cm [1⅜" × 23⅝"]
Cotton woven webbing (pouch zipper opening)
  - 2.5×51 cm [1" × 20⅛"]
Cord (within woven webbing, zipper opening)
  - 0.3×14 cm [⅛" ×5½"]
Fusible interfacing （gussets）

- 20×10 cm [7⅞" × 4"]
1 Zipper - 20 cm [7⅞"]
Embroidery floss - colors as desired

▶ Instructions
1. Using the diagrams below and the embroidery
pattern on the facing page, appliqué and embroider the pouch body.
2. With wrong sides together and batting in between, baste and quilt the pouch body and the
two gussets.
3. With wrong sides together, sew the gussets to

the pouch body. Bind the raw edges.
4. Sew the zipper to either side of the pouch opening.
5. Fold the woven webbing in half; pin through
the zipper tape; topstitch along the edge of the
webbing, leaving a loop at the end for a handle.
6. Feed the cord through the folded webbing.
Trim off the end of the cord even with the bag
opening, leaving a 0.7 [¼"] seam allowance. Turn
the ends of the webbing inside; blindstitch closed.
7. Make the zipper tab and sew the end of the zipper to finish.

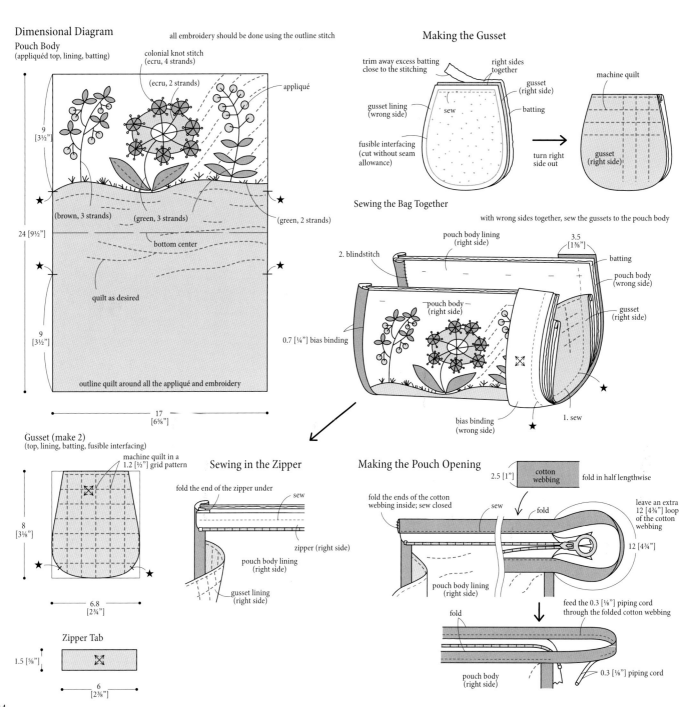

84

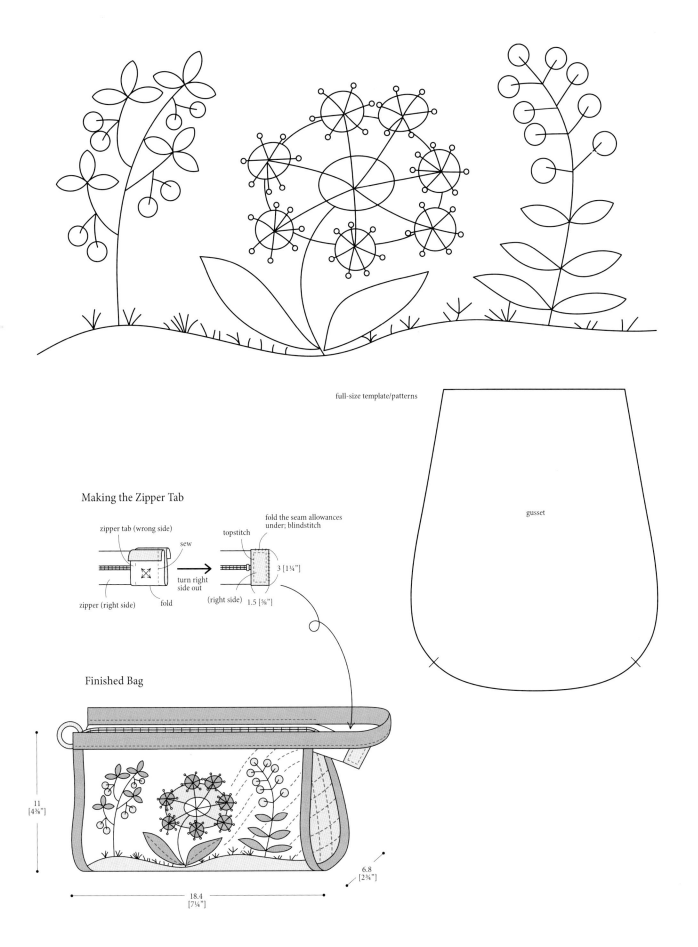

full-size template/patterns

gusset

Making the Zipper Tab

zipper tab (wrong side)

sew

topstitch

fold the seam allowances
under; blindstitch

turn right
side out

3 [1¼"]

zipper (right side)

fold

(right side)

1.5 [⅝"]

Finished Bag

11
[4⅜"]

6.8
[2¾"]

18.4
[7¼"]

12 Dots & Crosses Bag .... p.26 (full-size template/pattern - Side B of the pattern sheet insert)

► Materials Needed
Assorted fat quarters or scraps (pouch body, handles)
Homespun (bag opening)
 - 80×30 cm [31½" × 11¾"]
Homespun (bottom)
 - 15×25 cm [5⅞" × 9¾"]
Cotton print (lining) and Batting (each)
 - 110×45 cm [43¼" × 17¾"]
Muslin (bottom facing)
 - 25×15 cm [9¾" × 5⅞"]
Cotton woven webbing (handles)
 - 3×48 cm [1¼" × 18⅞"]
Lightweight fusible interfacing (bag opening)
 - 25×10 cm [9¾" × 4"]
Heavyweight fusible interfacing (bottom)
 - 25×25 cm [9¾" × 9¾"]

Fusible interfacing (handles)
 - 40×10 cm [15¾" × 4"]
Double-sided fusible interfacing (bottom)
 - 21×11 cm [8¼" × 4⅜"]

► Instructions
1. Using the diagrams below and the pattern, piece and appliqué the bag body front and back, including the appliquéd top bag opening.
2. Cut the lining of the bag body back with generous seams along the sides. With wrong sides together and batting in between, baste and quilt the front and back.
3. With right sides together, sew the side seams of the bag body front and back. Use the extra lining fabric from the bag body back along the side seams to bind the raw edges. Blindstitch down.

4. Make the bottom. Lay the wrong sides together with heavyweight fusible interfacing and batting in between, quilt the bag bottom and muslin facing. With right sides together, sew the bottom to the bottom bag opening.
5. Make the handles and baste in place.
6. Fuse heavyweight interfacing to the back of the bottom lining. Take a running stitch around the perimeter in the seam allowance; gather and tie off to turn the seam allowances under. Place double-sided interfacing between the quilted muslin facing on the bag bottom and the lining. Iron to set; blindstitch all the way around to secure.
7. Make the bag opening lining; sew side seams. With right sides together, align edges; sew. Snip into seam allowance; flip over, turn seams under and blindstitch down to finish.

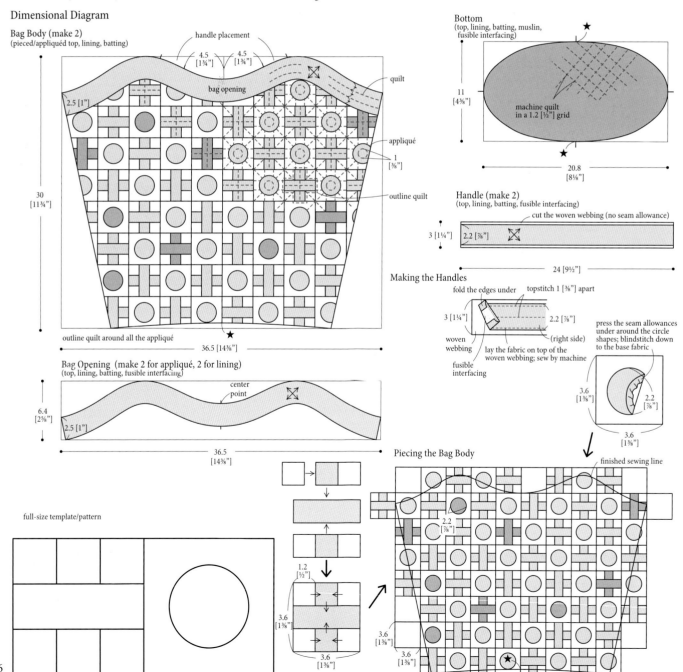

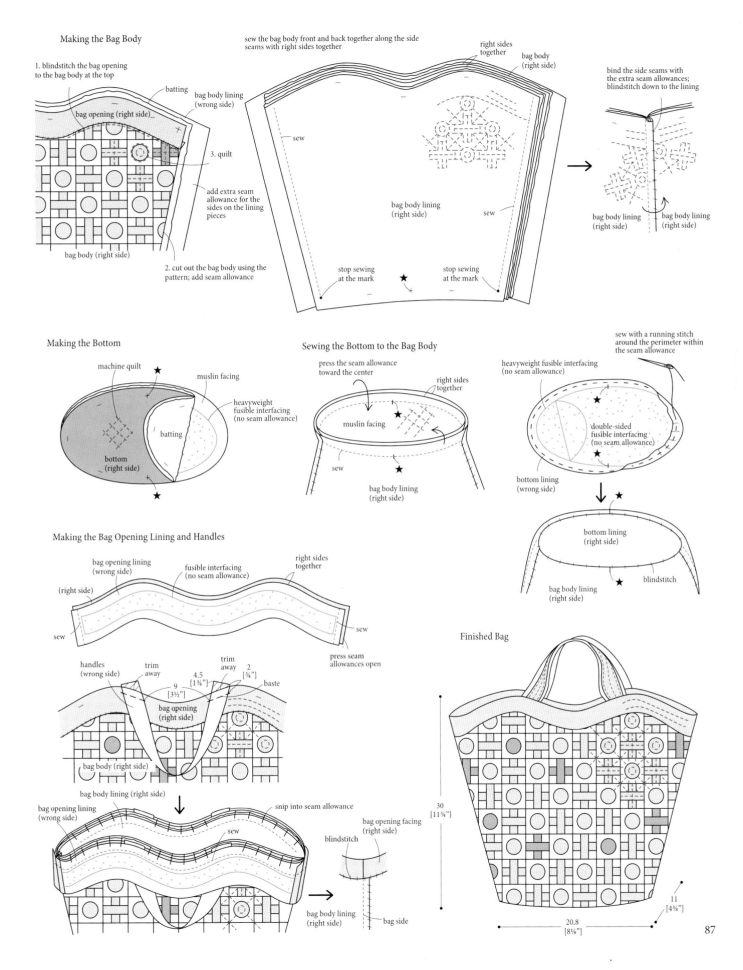

Making the Bag Body

sew the bag body front and back together along the side seams with right sides together

1. blindstitch the bag opening to the bag body at the top

batting

bag opening (right side)

bag body lining (wrong side)

3. quilt

add extra seam allowance for the sides on the lining pieces

bag body (right side)

2. cut out the bag body using the pattern; add seam allowance

right sides together

bag body (right side)

bag body lining (right side)

sew

sew

bag body lining (right side)

stop sewing at the mark

★

stop sewing at the mark

bind the side seams with the extra seam allowances; blindstitch down to the lining

bag body lining (right side)

bag body lining (right side)

Making the Bottom

machine quilt ★

muslin facing

batting

bottom (right side)

heavyweight fusible interfacing (no seam allowance)

★

Sewing the Bottom to the Bag Body

press the seam allowance toward the center

right sides together

muslin facing

sew

★

bag body lining (right side)

sew with a running stitch around the perimeter within the seam allowance

heavyweight fusible interfacing (no seam allowance)

★

double-sided fusible interfacing (no seam allowance)

★

bottom lining (wrong side)

bottom lining (right side)

bag body lining (right side)

★

blindstitch

Making the Bag Opening Lining and Handles

bag opening lining (wrong side)

fusible interfacing (no seam allowance)

right sides together

(right side)

sew

sew

press seam allowances open

handles (wrong side)

trim away

trim away

4.5 [1¾"]

9 [3½"]

2 [¾"]

baste

bag opening (right side)

bag body (right side)

bag body lining (right side)

bag opening lining (wrong side)

sew

snip into seam allowance

bag opening facing (right side)

blindstitch

bag body lining (right side)

bag side

Finished Bag

30 [11¾"]

11 [4⅜"]

20.8 [8⅛"]

13 Spinning Circles Shoulder Bag

--------- p.28   (full-size template/pattern - Side B of the pattern sheet insert)

► **Materials Needed**
Assorted fat quarters or scraps (appliqué)
Homespun (bag body front, back, gusset, bottom, flap facing, button cover)
 - 80×45 cm [31½" × 17¾"]
Cotton print (lining) and Batting (each)
 - 90×40 cm [35⅜" × 15¾"]
Muslin (flap facing)
 - 40×35 cm [15¾" × 13¾"]
Homespun (bias binding, seams)
 - 2.5×180 cm [1" ×71"] bias binding
Homespun Piping (bias binding for piping on flap)
 - 2.5×90 cm [1" ×35⅜"] bias binding
 - 0.4×90 cm [⅛" ×35⅜"] cord for inside piping
Cotton woven webbing (strap)
 - 3.8 × 105 cm [1½" ×41⅜"]

1 Magnetic closure button - 2 cm [¾"]
Fusible interfacing（gusset）
 - 75×5 cm [29½" × 2"]
Lightweight fusible interfacing (flap)
 - 80×40 cm [31½" × 15¾"]
Double-sided fusible interfacing (flap)

► **Instructions**
1. Using the diagram below and the pattern, piece the bag flap front. With wrong sides together and batting in between, quilt the pieced top and muslin facing.
2. Baste the piping around flap edge; with right sides together lay the flap lining on the pieced top; sew around the edge. Turn right side out; slip the double-sided fusible interface inside the flap; press.
3. Cut out the bag body front, back, and gusset; with wrong sides together and batting in between; quilt. Sew the darts in the front.
4. With right sides up, lay the bag flap on the top of the bag back; sew. Use the flap facing to cover the seam; topstitch to finish and secure.
5. Cut out the pieces for the gusset; with right sides together, sandwich the strap ends on both sides. Turn right side out; quilt the gusset.
6. With right sides together, sew the bag front and back to the gusset; bind the seams with the bias binding.
7. Sew the fabric-covered magnetic buttons to the bag front and the lining side of the flap to finish.

Dimensional Diagram

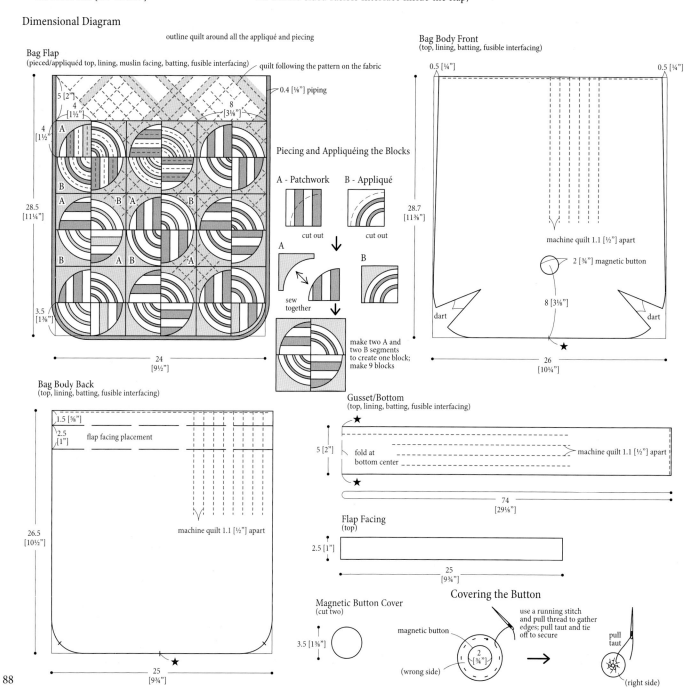

88

Making the Bag Flap

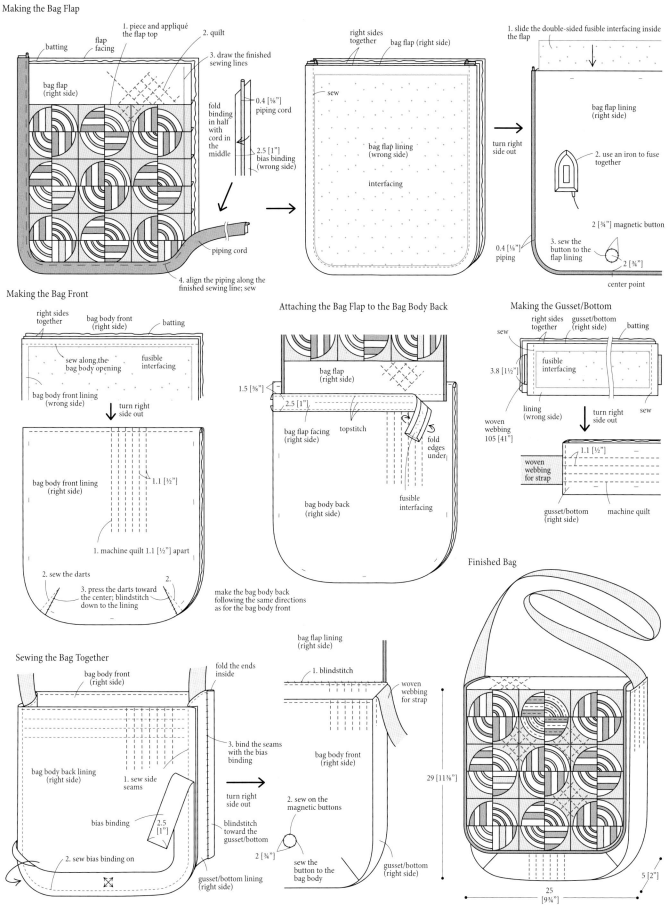

batting
flap facing
bag flap (right side)

1. piece and appliqué the flap top
2. quilt
3. draw the finished sewing lines

fold binding in half with cord in the middle

0.4 [⅛"] piping cord
2.5 [1"] bias binding (wrong side)

piping cord

4. align the piping along the finished sewing line; sew

right sides together
bag flap (right side)

sew

bag flap lining (wrong side)

bag flap lining (wrong side)

interfacing

turn right side out

1. slide the double-sided fusible interfacing inside the flap

bag flap lining (right side)

2. use an iron to fuse together

2 [¾"] magnetic button

3. sew the button to the flap lining

2 [¾"]

0.4 [⅛"] piping

center point

Making the Bag Front

right sides together
bag body front (right side)
batting

sew along the bag body opening
fusible interfacing

bag body front lining (wrong side)

turn right side out

bag body front lining (right side)

1.1 [½"]

1. machine quilt 1.1 [½"] apart

2. sew the darts

3. press the darts toward the center; blindstitch down to the lining

2.

Attaching the Bag Flap to the Bag Body Back

bag flap (right side)

1.5 [⅝"]
2.5 [1"]

bag flap facing (right side)
topstitch

fold edges under

bag body back (right side)

fusible interfacing

make the bag body back following the same directions as for the bag body front

Making the Gusset/Bottom

right sides together
gusset/bottom (right side)
batting

sew

3.8 [1½"]
fusible interfacing

woven webbing 105 [41"]
lining (wrong side)
sew

turn right side out

1.1 [1½"]

woven webbing for strap

gusset/bottom (right side)
machine quilt

Sewing the Bag Together

bag body front (right side)
fold the ends inside

bag body back lining (right side)

1. sew side seams

bias binding
2.5 [1"]

3. bind the seams with the bias binding

turn right side out

blindstitch toward the gusset/bottom

2. sew bias binding on

gusset/bottom lining (right side)

bag flap lining (right side)

1. blindstitch

woven webbing for strap

bag body front (right side)

2. sew on the magnetic buttons

2 [¾"]

sew the button to the bag body

gusset/bottom (right side)

Finished Bag

29 [11⅜"]

25 [9¾"]

5 [2"]

89

14 Pieced Blocks Shoulder Bag

...... p.30 (full-size template/pattern - Side B of the pattern sheet insert)

▶ Materials Needed
Assorted fat quarters or scraps (front piecing)
Homespun (bag body back, gusset, shoulder strap, flap facing, button cover, loop, tab)
  - 80×80 cm [31½" × 31½"]
Cotton print (lining) and Batting (each)
  - 80×70 cm [31½" × 27½"]
Fusible interfacing (bag body lining, gusset/shoulder strap) - 80×70 cm [31½" × 27½"]
Double-sided fusible interfacing (flap)
  - 40×35 cm [15¾" × 13¾"]
Muslin (flap facing)
  - 40×40 cm [15¾" × 15¾"]
Homespun Piping (bias binding for piping on flap)
  - 2.5×90 cm [1" × 35⅜"] bias binding
  - 0.4×90 cm [⅛" × 35⅜"] cord for inside piping
1 Zipper - 33 cm [13"]

1 Magnetic closure button - 2 cm [¾"]
D-ring hardware (loop) - 1 cm [⅜"]

▶ Instructions
1. Using the diagram below and the pattern, piece the bag flap front. With wrong sides together and batting in between, quilt the pieced top and muslin facing.
2. Baste the piping around flap edge; with right sides together lay the flap lining on the pieced top; sew around the edge. Turn right side out; slip the double-sided fusible interfacing inside the flap; press.
3. Cut out bag body; with wrong sides together and batting in between, baste and quilt the bag body. With right sides together, sew the zipper to the top

of the back area and to the top (bag opening) of the front (the bag will be in a cylinder shape).
4. With right sides up, lay the bag flap on the top of the bag back; sew. Use the flap facing to cover the seam; topstitch to finish and secure.
5. Cut out the pieces for the gusset/shoulder strap. With right sides together and batting on the back, sew around the edges, leaving an opening for turning. Turn right side out; quilt; blindstitch opening closed.
6. With wrong sides together, set in the gusset/shoulder strap (inserting loop), sew to the bag body using a ladder stitch. Add the decorative D-ring as shown.
7. Sew the fabric-covered magnetic buttons to the bag front and the lining side of the flap to finish.

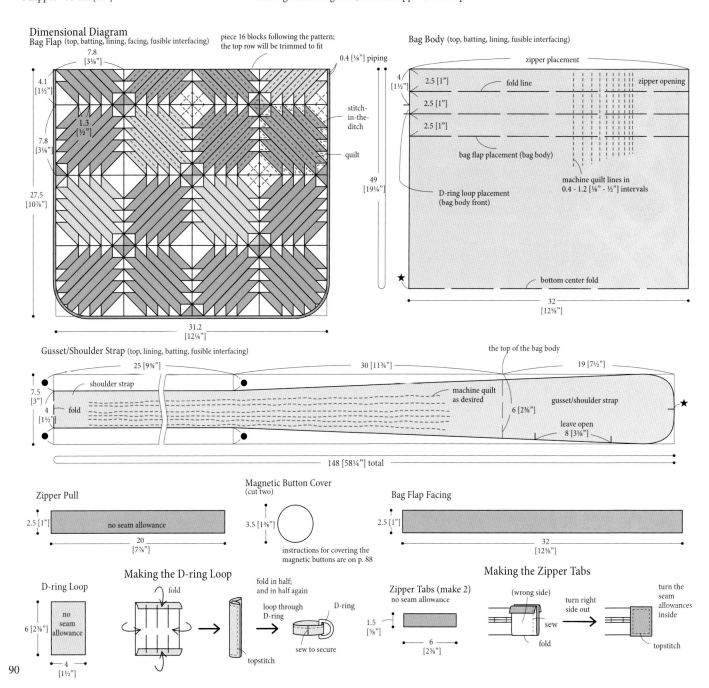

Dimensional Diagram
Bag Flap (top, batting, lining, facing, fusible interfacing)

piece 16 blocks following the pattern; the top row will be trimmed to fit

7.8 [3⅛"]
4.1 [1½"]
1.3 [½"]
7.8 [3⅛"]
27.5 [10⅞"]
31.2 [12¼"]

0.4 [⅛"] piping
stitch-in-the-ditch
quilt

Bag Body (top, batting, lining, fusible interfacing)

zipper placement
4 [1½"]
2.5 [1"] fold line
2.5 [1"]
2.5 [1"]
zipper opening
bag flap placement (bag body)
D-ring loop placement (bag body front)
machine quilt lines in 0.4 - 1.2 [⅛" - ½"] intervals
bottom center fold
49 [19¼"]
32 [12⅝"]

Gusset/Shoulder Strap (top, lining, batting, fusible interfacing)

the top of the bag body

25 [9¾"]
30 [11¾"]
19 [7½"]
7.5 [3"]
4 [1½"]
shoulder strap
fold
machine quilt as desired
gusset/shoulder strap
6 [2⅜"]
leave open 8 [3⅛"]
148 [58¼"] total

Zipper Pull
2.5 [1"]
no seam allowance
20 [7⅞"]

Magnetic Button Cover (cut two)
3.5 [1⅜"]
instructions for covering the magnetic buttons are on p. 88

Bag Flap Facing
2.5 [1"]
32 [12⅝"]

Making the D-ring Loop

D-ring Loop
no seam allowance
6 [2⅜"]
4 [1½"]

fold
fold in half; and in half again
loop through D-ring
D-ring
sew to secure
topstitch

Zipper Tabs (make 2)
no seam allowance
1.5 [⅝"]
6 [2⅜"]

Making the Zipper Tabs
(wrong side)
turn right side out
turn the seam allowances inside
sew
fold
topstitch

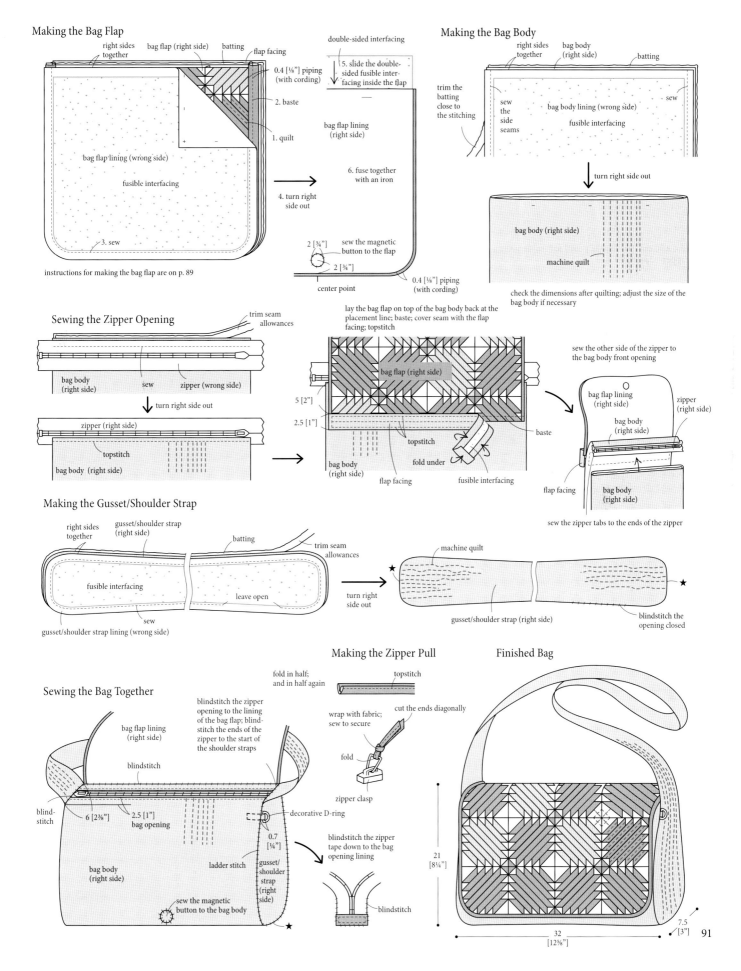

Making the Bag Flap

right sides together
bag flap (right side)
batting
flap facing
0.4 [⅛"] piping (with cording)
2. baste
1. quilt
bag flap lining (wrong side)
fusible interfacing
3. sew
4. turn right side out

double-sided interfacing
5. slide the double-sided fusible interfacing inside the flap
bag flap lining (right side)
6. fuse together with an iron
sew the magnetic button to the flap
2 [¾"]
2 [¾"]
center point
0.4 [⅛"] piping (with cording)

instructions for making the bag flap are on p. 89

Making the Bag Body

right sides together
bag body (right side)
batting
trim the batting close to the stitching
sew the side seams
bag body lining (wrong side)
fusible interfacing
sew
turn right side out

bag body (right side)
machine quilt

check the dimensions after quilting; adjust the size of the bag body if necessary

Sewing the Zipper Opening

trim seam allowances
bag body (right side)
sew
zipper (wrong side)
turn right side out
zipper (right side)
topstitch
bag body (right side)

lay the bag flap on top of the bag body back at the placement line; baste; cover seam with the flap facing; topstitch

bag flap (right side)
5 [2"]
2.5 [1"]
topstitch
fold under
bag body (right side)
flap facing
fusible interfacing
baste

sew the other side of the zipper to the bag body front opening

bag flap lining (right side)
zipper (right side)
bag body (right side)
flap facing
bag body (right side)

sew the zipper tabs to the ends of the zipper

Making the Gusset/Shoulder Strap

right sides together
gusset/shoulder strap (right side)
batting
trim seam allowances
fusible interfacing
leave open
sew
gusset/shoulder strap lining (wrong side)

turn right side out

machine quilt
★
gusset/shoulder strap (right side)
★
blindstitch the opening closed

Making the Zipper Pull

fold in half; and in half again
topstitch
wrap with fabric; sew to secure
cut the ends diagonally
fold
zipper clasp

Finished Bag

Sewing the Bag Together

bag flap lining (right side)
blindstitch the zipper opening to the lining of the bag flap; blindstitch the ends of the zipper to the start of the shoulder straps
blindstitch
blind-stitch
6 [2⅜"]
2.5 [1"]
bag opening
decorative D-ring
0.7 [¼"]
bag body (right side)
ladder stitch
gusset/ shoulder strap (right side)
sew the magnetic button to the bag body
★

blindstitch the zipper tape down to the bag opening lining
blindstitch

21 [8¼"]
32 [12⅝"]
7.5 [3"]

15 Patchwork Pencil Case ⠀⠀⠀⠀⠀ p.31

▶ Materials Needed

Assorted fat quarters or scraps (piecing, bottom, zipper tabs)
Muslin (pencil case facing)
 – 30×20 cm [11¾" × 7⅞"]
Cotton print (lining) and Batting (each)
 – 30×20 cm [11¾" × 7⅞"]
1 Zipper - 23 cm [9"]
1 Square metal purse frame (top zipper opening)
 – 0.3 × 6 × 18 cm [⅛" × 2⅜" × 7⅛"]

▶ Instructions

1. Using the diagrams below, piece the two pencil case body sections. Sew the bottom in between the two sections as shown.
2. With wrong sides together and batting in between, baste and quilt the pencil case body.
3. With right sides together, sew the side seams; fold with the side seam on top; sew across the open area to make the gussets. Topstitch the "v" on each side seam along the pencil case opening.
4. Sew the zipper in on each side of the pencil case opening.
5. Make the pencil case lining as shown.
6. With right sides together, place the pencil case body inside the lining. Sew from the finished "v" around one entire side to the other "v." Repeat for the other side, leaving an 8 cm [3⅛"] opening for turning. Turn the pencil case right side out; blindstitch opening closed.
7. Open the zipper. Sew two parallel lines, as shown, to make a channel. Insert the square metal purse frame pieces into the channel on each side. Blindstitch the "v" areas closed.
8. Sew the zipper tabs to each end of the zipper to finish.

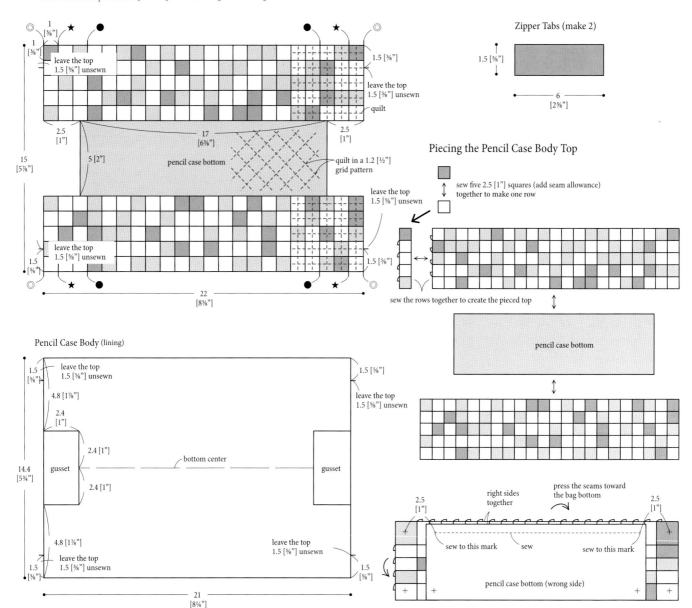

Dimensional Diagram
Pencil Case Body/Bottom (pieced top, bottom, batting, muslin facing)

Zipper Tabs (make 2)

Piecing the Pencil Case Body Top

Pencil Case Body (lining)

92

Sewing the Pencil Case Together

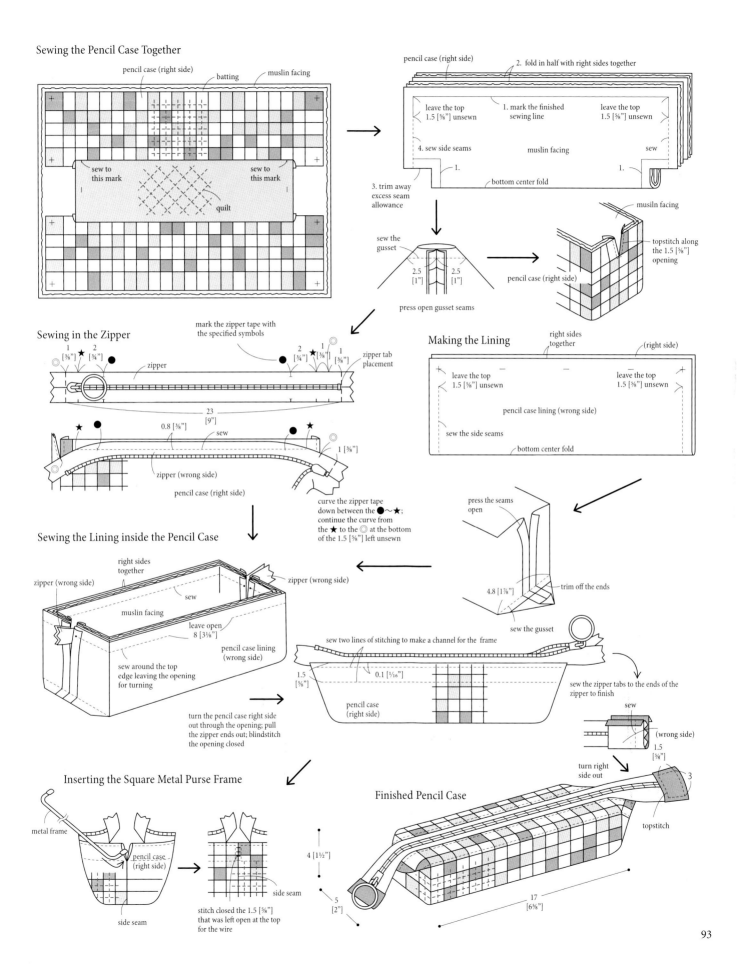

pencil case (right side) batting muslin facing

sew to this mark sew to this mark quilt

pencil case (right side)
2. fold in half with right sides together
leave the top 1.5 [⅝"] unsewn 1. mark the finished sewing line leave the top 1.5 [⅝"] unsewn
4. sew side seams muslin facing sew
1. bottom center fold 1.

3. trim away excess seam allowance

sew the gusset
2.5 [1"] 2.5 [1"]
press open gusset seams

musiln facing
topstitch along the 1.5 [⅝"] opening
pencil case (right side)

Sewing in the Zipper

mark the zipper tape with the specified symbols

1 [⅜"] 2 [¾"] ● 2 [¾"] ★ [⅜"] 1 [⅜"] ◎ zipper tab placement
zipper
23 [9"]

★ ● 0.8 [⅜"] sew ● ★ ◎ 1 [⅜"]
zipper (wrong side)
pencil case (right side)

curve the zipper tape down between the ●~★; continue the curve from the ★ to the ◎ at the bottom of the 1.5 [⅝"] left unsewn

Making the Lining

right sides together (right side)
leave the top 1.5 [⅝"] unsewn leave the top 1.5 [⅝"] unsewn
pencil case lining (wrong side)
sew the side seams
bottom center fold

press the seams open
4.8 [1⅞"] trim off the ends
sew the gusset

Sewing the Lining inside the Pencil Case

zipper (wrong side) right sides together sew zipper (wrong side)
muslin facing
leave open 8 [3⅛"]
pencil case lining (wrong side)
sew around the top edge leaving the opening for turning

turn the pencil case right side out through the opening; pull the zipper ends out; blindstitch the opening closed

sew two lines of stitching to make a channel for the frame
1.5 [⅝"] 0.1 [¹⁄₁₆"]
pencil case (right side)

sew the zipper tabs to the ends of the zipper to finish
sew (wrong side)
1.5 [⅝"]
turn right side out 3
topstitch

Inserting the Square Metal Purse Frame

metal frame
pencil case (right side)
side seam side seam
stitch closed the 1.5 [⅝"] that was left open at the top for the wire

4 [1½"]
5 [2"]

Finished Pencil Case

17 [6⅝"]

16 Perfect Little Pouchette

······· *p.32*   (full-size template/pattern - Side B of the pattern sheet insert)

▶ Materials Needed
Assorted fat quarters or scraps (bag body piecing)
Cotton print (lining) and Batting (each)
 - 60×30 cm [23⅜" × 11¾"]
Homespun (bias binding)
 - 3.5×50 cm [1⅜" × 19¾"] (bag opening)
Homespun (bias binding for seams)
 - 2.5×60 cm [1" × 23⅜"]
Waxed cord (button loop)
 - 0.3×8 cm [⅛" × 3⅛"]
Flat cord (side strap loops)
 - 0.5×10 cm [¼" × 3⅛"] (cut in half for two)
1 Decorative button - 2 cm [¾"]
2 Swivel clasp hardware (strap)

Woven webbing (shoulder strap)
 - 2.5×140 cm [1" × 55⅛"]

Fusible interfacing (button loop) - scrap

▶ Instructions
1. Using the diagram below and the pattern, piece the four bag body sections. Cut out the lining pieces with excess seam allowance along the center seam to use for binding. With wrong sides together and batting in between, baste and quilt the segments.
2. With right sides together, sew the front A and B segments together along the center seam. Repeat for the back C and D segments. Trim the ex-

cess seam allowances down including one of the excess lining seam allowances. Use the leftover seam allowance to bind the raw edges.
3. Baste the side strap loops in place on the front A/B. With right sides together, sew the body front and back seams. Bind the seams with the bias binding.
4. Bind the bag opening with the shorter bias binding.
5. Sew the button loop/tab and button to the bag front.
6. Make the shoulder strap as shown. Clip the strap to the bag through the side strap loops to finish.

Dimensional Diagram
(pieced top, batting, lining for each; cut the center lining generously to use for binding the center seams)

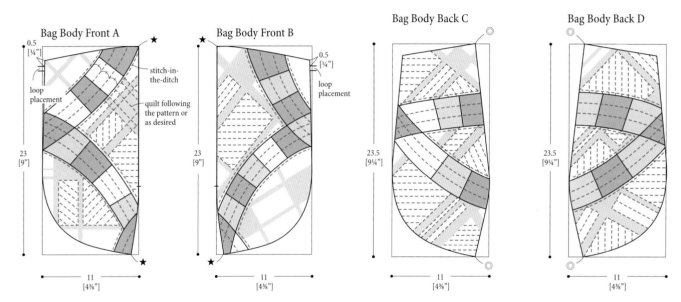

Piecing the Bag Body A-D

trace the pieces from the pattern sheet; mark each number clearly on each one; add seam allowances before cutting out

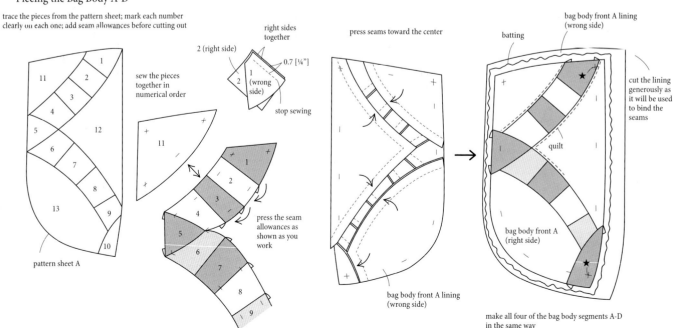

make all four of the bag body segments A-D in the same way

Sewing the Front A/B and Back C/D Pieces Together

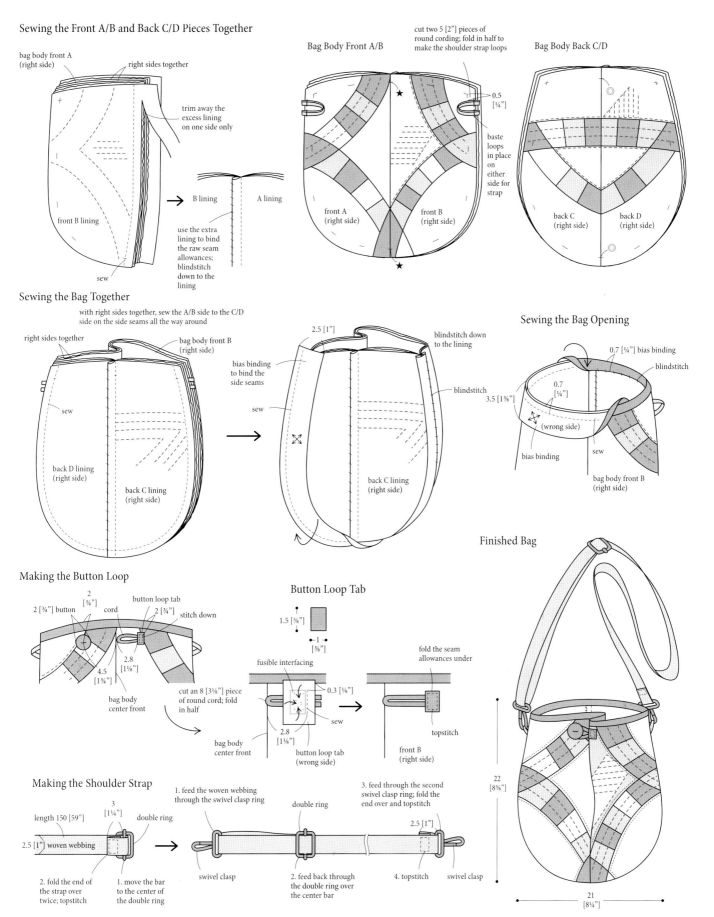

bag body front A
(right side)

right sides together

trim away the excess lining on one side only

front B lining

sew

B lining · A lining

use the extra lining to bind the raw seam allowances; blindstitch down to the lining

Bag Body Front A/B

cut two 5 [2"] pieces of round cording; fold in half to make the shoulder strap loops

0.5 [¼"]

baste loops in place on either side for strap

front A (right side)

front B (right side)

Bag Body Back C/D

back C (right side)

back D (right side)

Sewing the Bag Together

with right sides together, sew the A/B side to the C/D side on the side seams all the way around

right sides together

bag body front B (right side)

sew

back D lining (right side)

back C lining (right side)

2.5 [1"]

bias binding to bind the side seams

sew

blindstitch down to the lining

blindstitch

back C lining (right side)

Sewing the Bag Opening

0.7 [¼"] bias binding

blindstitch

0.7 [¼"]

3.5 [1⅜"]

(wrong side)

bias binding

sew

bag body front B (right side)

Making the Button Loop

2 [¾"]

2 [¾"] button

button loop tab

cord

2 [¾"]

stitch down

2.8 [1⅛"]

4.5 [1¾"]

bag body center front

cut an 8 [3⅛"] piece of round cord; fold in half

Button Loop Tab

1.5 [⅝"]

1 [⅜"]

fusible interfacing

0.3 [⅛"]

sew

2.8 [1⅛"]

bag body center front

button loop tab (wrong side)

fold the seam allowances under

topstitch

front B (right side)

Finished Bag

22 [8⅝"]

21 [8¼"]

Making the Shoulder Strap

length 150 [59"]

3 [1¼"]

double ring

2.5 [1"] woven webbing

2. fold the end of the strap over twice; topstitch

1. move the bar to the center of the double ring

1. feed the woven webbing through the swivel clasp ring

double ring

swivel clasp

2. feed back through the double ring over the center bar

3. feed through the second swivel clasp ring; fold the end over and topstitch

2.5 [1"]

4. topstitch

swivel clasp

95

17 Little House Tea Cozy

······· *p.34* (enlarge template/pattern by 200% - Side B of the pattern sheet insert)

▶ Materials Needed
Assorted fat quarters or scraps (appliqué, loop handle)
Cotton print (background)
  – 30×75 cm [11¾" × 29½"]
Homespun (lining) and Batting (each)
  – 35×75 cm [13¾" × 29½"]
Fusible interfacing (loop handle) - scrap

▶ Instructions
1. Using the diagram below and the pattern (enlarge on a copy machine by 200%), piece, appliqué, and embroider the background fabric for all three sides of the tea cozy body.
2. With right sides together, lay the back and front on top of the batting. Sew around the outside leaving an 8 cm [3⅛"] opening for turning along the bottom. Turn each one right side out; blindstitch opening closed. Baste and quilt each piece.
3. With wrong sides together, sew the three pieces together along the side seams using a ladder stitch.
4. Topstitch by machine along each side from top to bottom along all three sides.
5. Make the button loop handle. Fold it in half and blindstitch to the very top of the roof to finish.

Dimensional Diagram

Tea Cozy Body A (make 1)
(top, batting, lining)

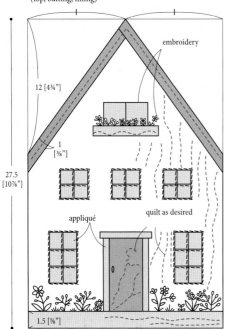

Tea Cozy Body B (make 2)
(top, batting, lining)

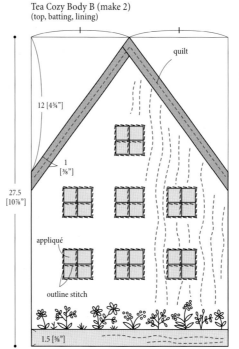

Tea Cozy Loop Handle

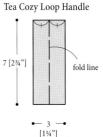

outline stitch around all piecing, appliqué, and embroidery

Outline Stitch

Embroidery

lazy daisy stitch (pink, 3 strands)
French knot stitch (mustard, 3 strands)
outline stitch (moss green, 2 strands)
lazy daisy stitch (olive green, 3 strands)
French knot stitch (orange, 3 strands)
outline stitch (brown, 2 strands)

French Knot Stitch

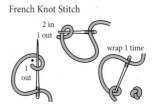

Lazy Daisy Stitch

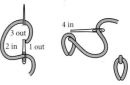

Bullion Stitch

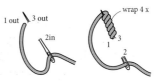

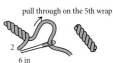

96

Putting the Tea Cozy Together

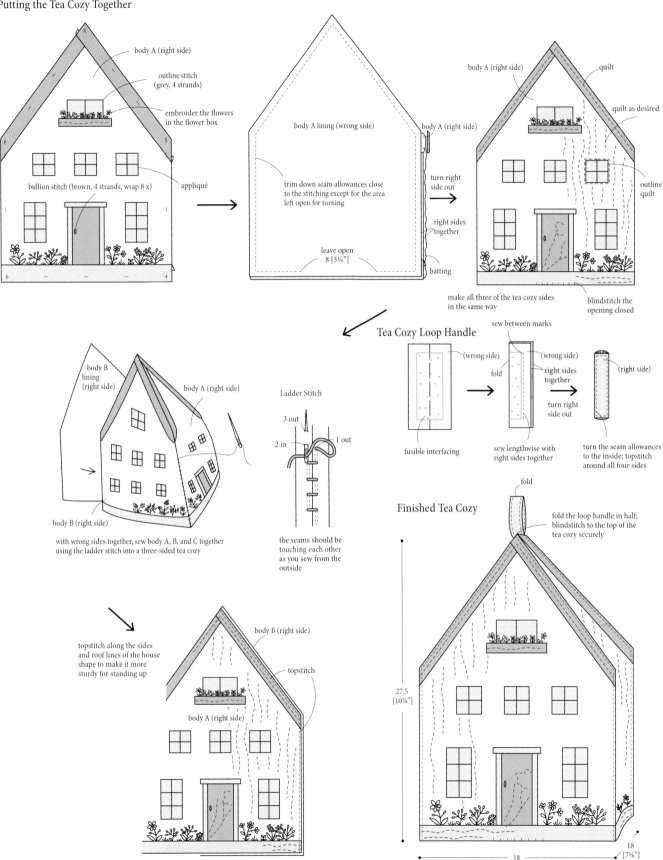

body A (right side)

outline stitch
(grey, 4 strands)

embroider the flowers
in the flower box

bullion stitch (brown, 4 strands, wrap 8 x)

appliqué

body A lining (wrong side)

body A (right side)

trim down seam allowances close
to the stitching except for the area
left open for turning

leave open
8 [3⅛"]

turn right
side out

right sides
together

batting

body A (right side)

quilt

quilt as desired

outline
quilt

make all three of the tea cozy sides
in the same way

blindstitch the
opening closed

body B
lining
(right side)

body A (right side)

body B (right side)

with wrong sides together, sew body A, B, and C together
using the ladder stitch into a three-sided tea cozy

Ladder Stitch

3 out

2 in

1 out

the seams should be
touching each other
as you sew from the
outside

Tea Cozy Loop Handle

sew between marks

(wrong side)

fold

(wrong side)

right sides
together

(right side)

turn right
side out

fusible interfacing

sew lengthwise with
right sides together

turn the seam allowances
to the inside; topstitch
around all four sides

Finished Tea Cozy

fold

fold the loop handle in half;
blindstitch to the top of the
tea cozy securely

27.5
[10⅞"]

18
[7⅛"]

18
[7⅛"]

topstitch along the sides
and roof lines of the house
shape to make it more
sturdy for standing up

body B (right side)

topstitch

body A (right side)

18·19 House-Shaped Placemats (1 & 2)

······ p.34 (enlarge template/pattern by 200% - Side B of the pattern sheet insert)

▶ Materials Needed
Assorted fat quarters or scraps (background, appliqué)
Cotton print (lining)
 – 35×45 cm [13¾" × 17¾"]
Lightweight fusible batting
 – 35×45 cm [13¾" × 17¾"]
Embroidery floss - colors as desired

▶ Instructions
1. Using the diagram below and the pattern (enlarge on a copy machine by 200%), piece, appliqué, and embroider the background fabric for either or both of the placemats.
2. With right sides together and batting in between, sew around the outside leaving a 10 cm [4"] opening for turning along the bottom. Turn right side out; blindstitch opening closed. Baste and quilt each piece to finish.

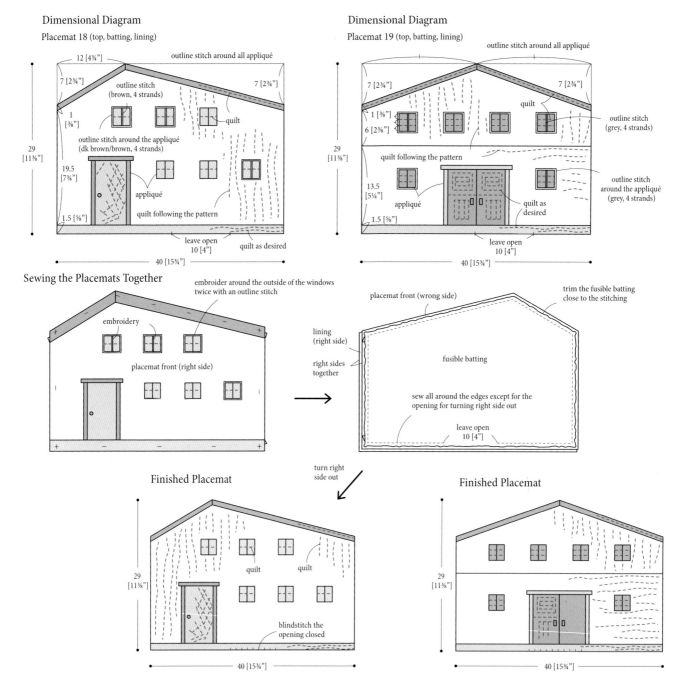

Dimensional Diagram
Placemat 18 (top, batting, lining)

outline stitch around all appliqué

12 [4¾"]
7 [2¾"]
7 [2¾"]
outline stitch (brown, 4 strands)
quilt
1 [⅜"]
outline stitch around the appliqué (dk brown/brown, 4 strands)
29 [11⅜"]
19.5 [7¾"]
appliqué
quilt following the pattern
1.5 [⅝"]
leave open 10 [4"]
quilt as desired
40 [15¾"]

Dimensional Diagram
Placemat 19 (top, batting, lining)

outline stitch around all appliqué

7 [2¾"]
7 [2¾"]
quilt
1 [⅜"]
6 [2⅜"]
outline stitch (grey, 4 strands)
29 [11⅜"]
quilt following the pattern
13.5 [5¼"]
appliqué
quilt as desired
outline stitch around the appliqué (grey, 4 strands)
1.5 [⅝"]
leave open 10 [4"]
40 [15¾"]

Sewing the Placemats Together

embroider around the outside of the windows twice with an outline stitch
embroidery
placemat front (right side)

placemat front (wrong side)
trim the fusible batting close to the stitching
lining (right side)
right sides together
fusible batting
sew all around the edges except for the opening for turning right side out
leave open 10 [4"]

Finished Placemat

turn right side out
29 [11⅜"]
quilt
quilt
blindstitch the opening closed
40 [15¾"]

Finished Placemat

29 [11⅜"]
40 [15¾"]

20 Cityscape Tablecloth

··· p.34 (enlarge template/pattern by 195% - Side B of the pattern sheet insert)

► Materials Needed
Assorted fat quarters or scraps (appliqué)
Homespun (tablecloth background)
 - 110×110 cm [43¼" × 43¼"]
Homespun (bias binding)
 - 3.5×470 cm [1⅜" ×185"]
Embroidery floss - colors as desired

► Instructions
1. Using the diagram below and the pattern (enlarge on a copy machine by 195%), appliqué and embroider the background fabric around all four sides.
2. Use a machine to topstitch around the perimeter of each house.
3. Bind the outside edge to finish.

Dimensional Diagram

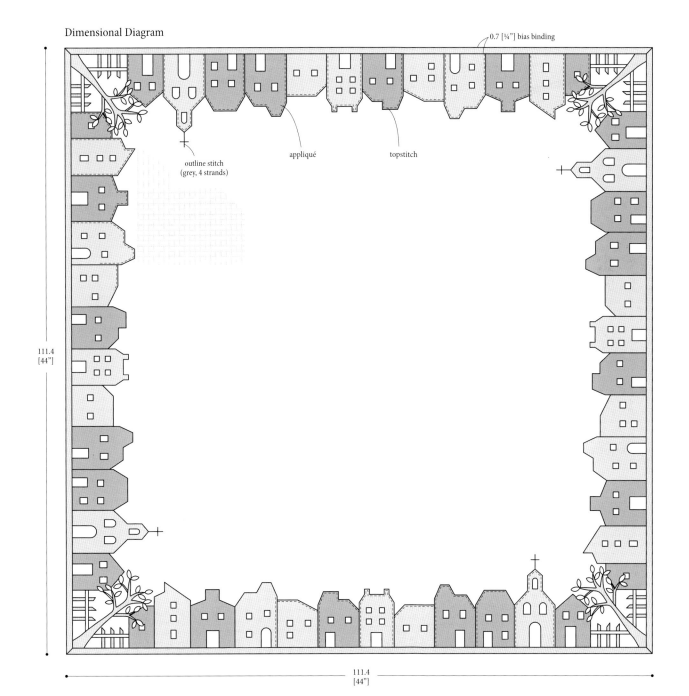

0.7 [¼"] bias binding

outline stitch
(grey, 4 strands)

appliqué

topstitch

111.4
[44"]

111.4
[44"]

▶ Materials Needed
Assorted fat quarters or scraps (piecing, bottom, box pull)
Homespun (lining) and Batting (each)
- 50×40 cm [19¾"× 15¾"]
Homespun (bias binding, seams)
- 2.5×70 cm [1"× 27½"] bias binding
Homespun Piping (bias binding for piping)
- 2.5×70 cm [1"× 27½"] bias binding
- 0.3×70 cm [⅛"× 27½"] cord for inside piping
Heavyweight fusible interfacing (bottom)
- 13×20 cm [5⅛"× 7⅞"]

Fusible interfacing（box pull）- scrap

▶ Instructions
1. Using the diagram below, piece the box front, back, and sides.
2. Sew the box front, back, and side pieces to the bottom. Cut out the entire lining. With wrong sides together and batting in between, baste and quilt the box body. Trim the lining and batting down as shown, leaving a generous seam allowance for the sides to use to bind the inside cor-

ners.
3. Make the inner bottom; topstitch to the bottom.
4. With right sides together, align the sides and front and back; use the excess seam allowance to bind the edges. Turn right side out.
5. Use the piping to bind the box opening, blindstitching it to the inside lining.
6. Make the box pulls; sew them to the box body front to finish.

Make both boxes in the same manner.

Dimensional Diagram   cut the batting and lining as one large piece, then trim to box shape

Fabric Box 2 Front and Back (22) (top)

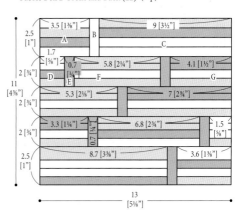

Fabric Box 2 Side (22) - (make 2) (top)

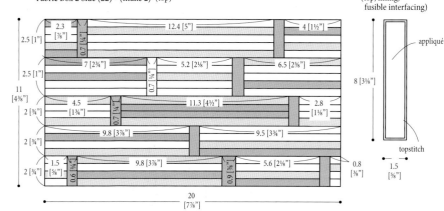

Box Pull
(top, lining,
fusible interfacing)

Fabric Box 1 Front and Back (21) (top)

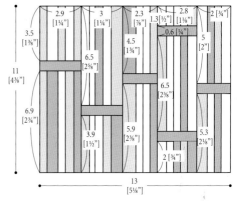

Fabric Box 1 Side (21) - (top) (make 2)

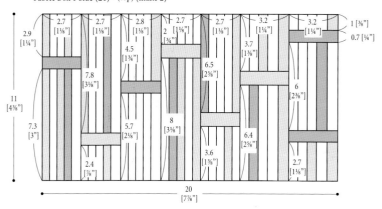

Fabric Box 2 Bottom/Inner Bottom Lining (22) (top, fusible interfacing)

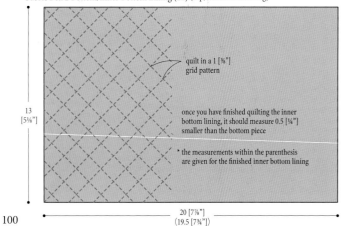

quilt in a 1 [⅜"] grid pattern

once you have finished quilting the inner bottom lining, it should measure 0.5 [¼"] smaller than the bottom piece

* the measurements within the parenthesis are given for the finished inner bottom lining

Fabric Box 1 Bottom/Inner Bottom Lining (21) (top, fusible interfacing)

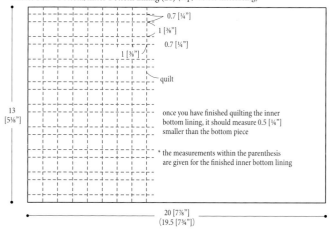

quilt

once you have finished quilting the inner bottom lining, it should measure 0.5 [¼"] smaller than the bottom piece

* the measurements within the parenthesis are given for the finished inner bottom lining

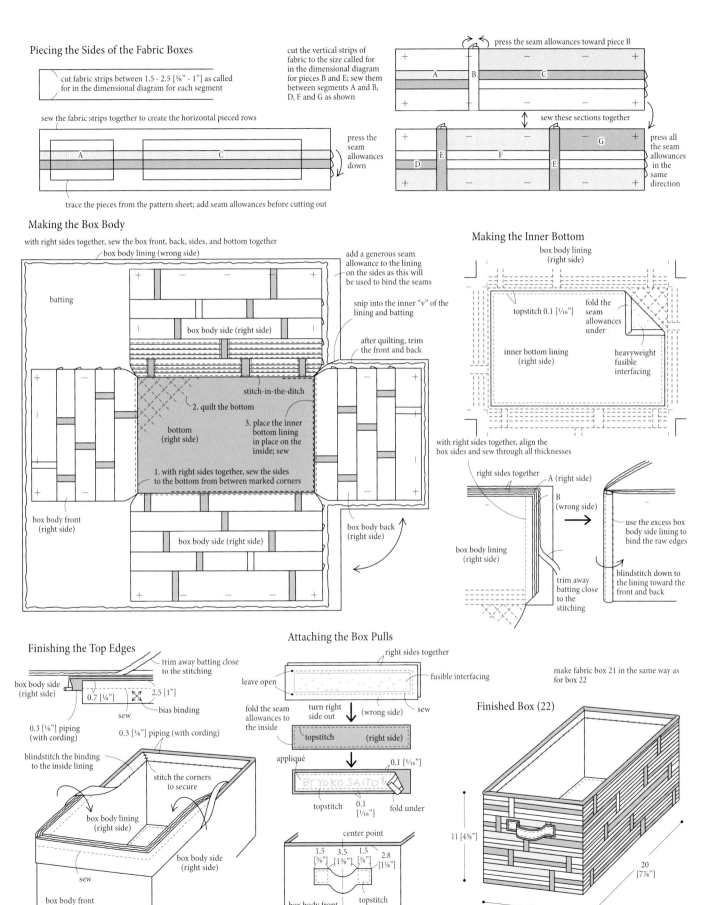

Piecing the Sides of the Fabric Boxes

cut fabric strips between 1.5 - 2.5 [⅝" - 1"] as called for in the dimensional diagram for each segment

cut the vertical strips of fabric to the size called for in the dimensional diagram for pieces B and E; sew them between segments A and B, D, F and G as shown

press the seam allowances toward piece B

sew the fabric strips together to create the horizontal pieced rows

press the seam allowances down

sew these sections together

press all the seam allowances in the same direction

trace the pieces from the pattern sheet; add seam allowances before cutting out

Making the Box Body

with right sides together, sew the box front, back, sides, and bottom together

box body lining (wrong side)

add a generous seam allowance to the lining on the sides as this will be used to bind the seams

snip into the inner "v" of the lining and batting

after quilting, trim the front and back

batting

box body side (right side)

stitch-in-the-ditch

2. quilt the bottom

3. place the inner bottom lining in place on the inside; sew

bottom (right side)

1. with right sides together, sew the sides to the bottom from between marked corners

box body front (right side)

box body side (right side)

box body back (right side)

Making the Inner Bottom

box body lining (right side)

topstitch 0.1 [1/16"]

fold the seam allowances under

inner bottom lining (right side)

heavyweight fusible interfacing

with right sides together, align the box sides and sew through all thicknesses

right sides together

A (right side)

B (wrong side)

box body lining (right side)

trim away batting close to the stitching

use the excess box body side lining to bind the raw edges

blindstitch down to the lining toward the front and back

Finishing the Top Edges

trim away batting close to the stitching

box body side (right side)

0.7 [¼"]   2.5 [1"]

sew

bias binding

0.3 [⅛"] piping (with cording)

0.3 [⅛"] piping (with cording)

blindstitch the binding to the inside lining

stitch the corners to secure

box body lining (right side)

box body side (right side)

sew

box body front (right side)

Attaching the Box Pulls

right sides together

leave open

fusible interfacing

fold the seam allowances to the inside

turn right side out

(wrong side)

sew

topstitch   (right side)

appliqué

0.1 [1/16"]

BY YOKO SAITO

topstitch   0.1 [1/16"]   fold under

center point

1.5 [⅝"] 3.5 [1⅜"] 1.5 [⅝"] 2.8 [1⅛"]

box body front (right side)

topstitch

make fabric box 21 in the same way as for box 22

Finished Box (22)

11 [4⅜"]

20 [7⅞"]

13 [5⅛"]

101

23 Scissors Holder

·······› *p.38* (full-size template/pattern - Side B of the pattern sheet insert)

▶ Materials Needed
Assorted fat quarters or scraps (appliqué, tab)
Homespun (bag body, zipper opening, gusset)
 - 50×50 cm [19¾" × 19¾"]
Homespun (lining) and Batting (each)
 - 50×50 cm [19¾" × 19¾"]
Heavyweight fusible interfacing (bag body)
 - 15×30 cm [5⅞" × 11¾"]
Fusible interfacing (zipper opening, gusset)
 - 10×70 cm [4" × 27½"]
Homespun (bias binding, seams)
 - 2.5×130 cm [1" × 51¼"] bias binding
Cotton woven webbing (handle)
 - 1.5×40 cm [⅝" × 15¾"]
Ribbon (handle)

 - 1.5×40 cm [⅝" × 15¾"]
1 Zipper - 20 cm [7⅞"]

▶ Instructions
1. Using the diagram below and the pattern, piece, appliqué, and embroider the bag front sections. Cut out the lining pieces with excess seam allowance along the center to use for binding the seams. With wrong sides together and batting in between, baste and quilt. With right sides together, sew along the center seam; trim the excess seam allowance except for the lining and use that to bind the raw edges on both sides.
2. Make the bag body back in the same manner.
3. Sew the zipper to the zipper opening fabric as

shown.
4. With right sides together, sew the gusset to one end of the zipper opening; turn right side out; machine quilt leaving the opposite end with room for seam allowance. After quilting the gusset/zipper opening, turn the ends under and attach to the other end of the zipper opening; topstitch.
5. Make two handles by sewing the ribbon to the top of the woven webbing with a topstitch along the edges. Baste with right sides together to the top of the bag back and front.
6. With right sides together, sew the front and back to the zipper opening/gusset. Bind the raw edges with the bias binding to finish.

Dimensional Diagram

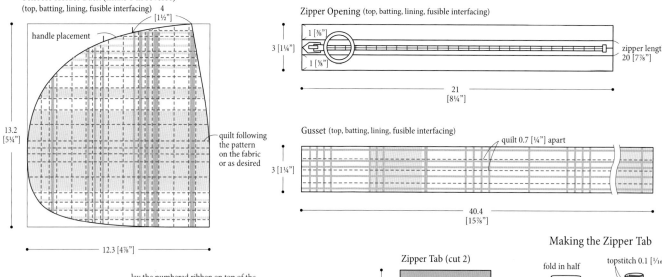

Scissors Holder Front A (top, batting, lining, facing)
handle placement
4 [1½"]
(lt grey, 3 strands)
(lt grey, 4 strands)
(lt grey, 2 strands)
(black, 3 strands)
appliqué
FISKARS
quilt following the pattern on the fabric or as desired
(grey, 2 strands)
satin stitch (grey, 3 strands)
13.2 [5¼"]
12.3 [4⅞"]

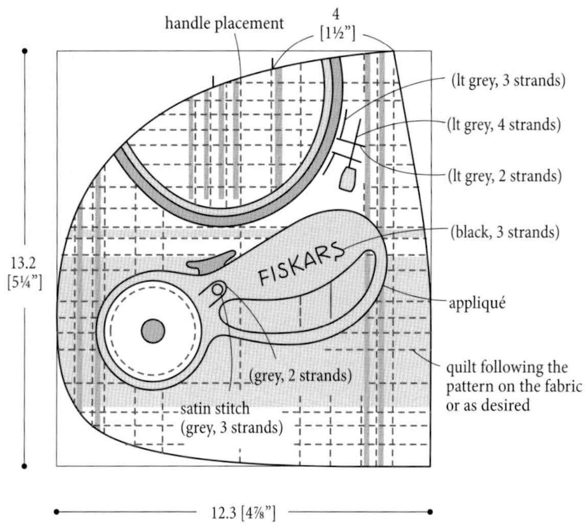

Scissors Holder Front B (top, batting, lining)
4 [1½"]
handle placement
use an outline stitch for all embroidery unless otherwise specified; add a generous seam allowance to the center front of both the front and back pieces as this will be used to bind the seams
satin stitch (grey, 3 strands)
appliqué
satin stitch (grey, 3 strands)
quilt following the pattern on the fabric or as desired
(black, 3 strands)
outline stitch around all appliqué and embroidery
13.2 [5¼"]
12.3 [4⅞"]

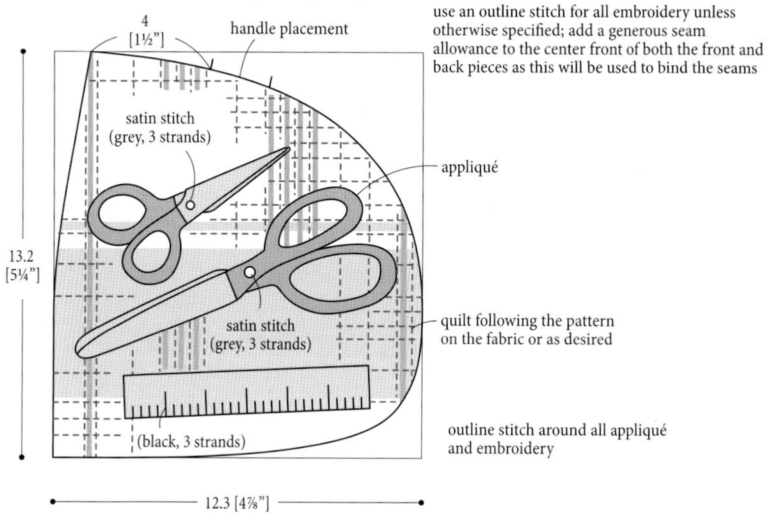

Scissors Holder Back (make 1 in reverse)
(top, batting, lining, fusible interfacing) 4 [1½"]
handle placement
quilt following the pattern on the fabric or as desired
13.2 [5¼"]
12.3 [4⅞"]

Zipper Opening (top, batting, lining, fusible interfacing)
1 [⅜"]
3 [1¼"]
1 [⅜"]
zipper length 20 [7⅞"]
21 [8¼"]

Gusset (top, batting, lining, fusible interfacing)
quilt 0.7 [¼"] apart
3 [1¼"]
40.4 [15⅞"]

Handles (make 2)
lay the numbered ribbon on top of the woven webbing to make each handle
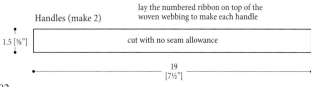
1.5 [⅝"]
cut with no seam allowance
19 [7½"]

Zipper Tab (cut 2)
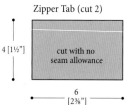
4 [1½"]
cut with no seam allowance
6 [2⅜"]

Making the Zipper Tab
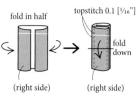
fold in half
topstitch 0.1 [¹⁄₁₆"]
fold down
(right side)
(right side)

102

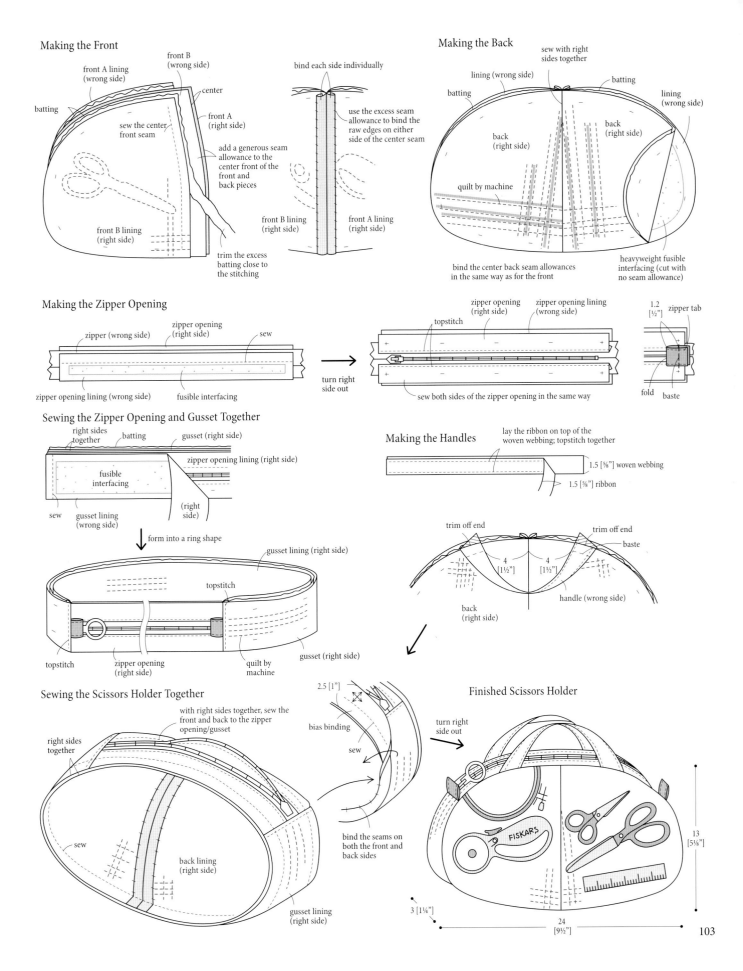

Making the Front

front A lining (wrong side)

batting

front B (wrong side)

center

front A (right side)

sew the center front seam

add a generous seam allowance to the center front of the front and back pieces

front B lining (right side)

trim the excess batting close to the stitching

bind each side individually

use the excess seam allowance to bind the raw edges on either side of the center seam

front B lining (right side)

front A lining (right side)

Making the Back

sew with right sides together

lining (wrong side)

batting

batting

lining (wrong side)

back (right side)

back (right side)

quilt by machine

heavyweight fusible interfacing (cut with no seam allowance)

bind the center back seam allowances in the same way as for the front

Making the Zipper Opening

zipper (wrong side)

zipper opening (right side)

sew

zipper opening lining (wrong side)

fusible interfacing

turn right side out

zipper opening (right side)

topstitch

zipper opening lining (wrong side)

sew both sides of the zipper opening in the same way

1.2 [½"]

zipper tab

fold

baste

Sewing the Zipper Opening and Gusset Together

right sides together

batting

gusset (right side)

fusible interfacing

zipper opening lining (right side)

sew

gusset lining (wrong side)

(right side)

form into a ring shape

gusset lining (right side)

topstitch

topstitch

zipper opening (right side)

quilt by machine

gusset (right side)

Making the Handles

lay the ribbon on top of the woven webbing; topstitch together

1.5 [⅝"] woven webbing

1.5 [⅝"] ribbon

trim off end

trim off end

baste

4 [1½"]

4 [1½"]

back (right side)

handle (wrong side)

Sewing the Scissors Holder Together

right sides together

with right sides together, sew the front and back to the zipper opening/gusset

sew

back lining (right side)

gusset lining (right side)

2.5 [1"]

bias binding

sew

bind the seams on both the front and back sides

turn right side out

Finished Scissors Holder

FISKARS

13 [5⅛"]

3 [1¼"]

24 [9½"]

Sewing Case

⌐- - - - - ⟍ p.38 (full-size template/pattern - Side B of the pattern sheet insert)

▶ Materials Needed
Assorted fat quarters or scraps (appliqué, back ground)
Homespun (lining, inner pockets, lid and bottom) - 110×25 cm [43¼" × 9¾"]
Batting
  - 40×30 cm [15¾" × 11¾"]
Heavyweight fusible interfacing (case body)
  - 15×20 cm [5⅞" × 7⅞"]
Fusible interfacing (zipper opening, gusset)
  - 10×70 cm [4" × 27½"]
1 Metal rectangle purse frame
  - 15×7 cm [5⅞" × 2¾"]
1 Wooden bead (purse frame charm)

Waxed cord (to attach charm)
  - 0.1×10 cm [¹/₁₆" × 4"]
Embroidery floss - colors as desired
▶ Instructions
1. Using the diagram below and the pattern, piece, appliqué, and embroider the case body. With right sides together, lay the case body and lining on top of the batting; sew around the edges leaving an opening at the bottom for turning. Turn right side out; sew the opening closed and quilt.
2. Make the case side in the same manner.
3. Make all the inner pockets A, B, C, and D. Blindstitch inner pockets A and C to the right

side of the case side lining; sew down the center of pocket C.
4. Topstitch inner pocket D to the inner lid; fold the bottom under and place on the case body lining. Blindstitch inner pocket B to the center of the case body section and sew down the center.
5. Blindstitch the inner bottom to the case body lining.
6. Sew the case body and the case sides together using a ladder stitch at the sides and around the bottom.
7. Attach the metal purse frame to the sewing case to finish.

Dimensional Diagram

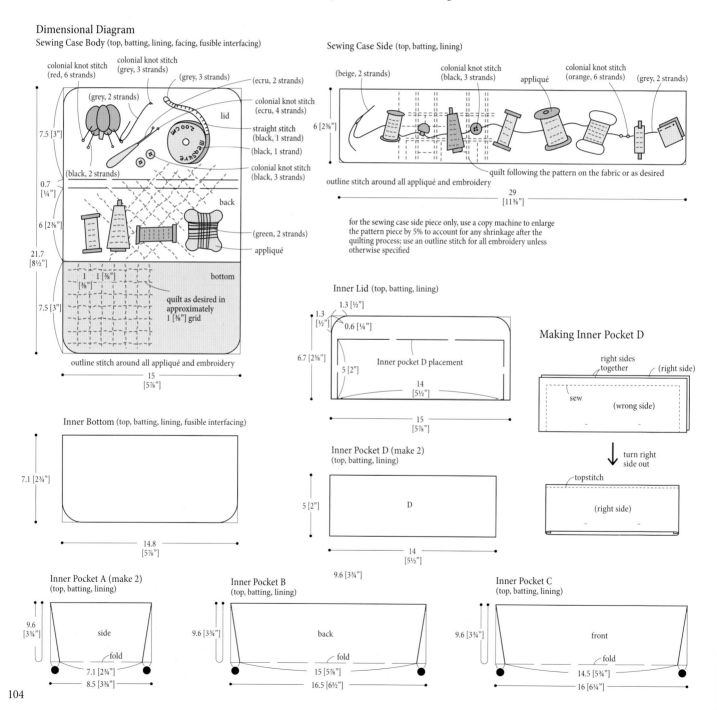

104

Making the Sewing Case Body

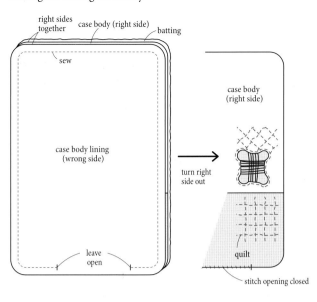

right sides together
case body (right side)
batting
sew
case body lining (wrong side)
leave open
turn right side out
case body (right side)
quilt
stitch opening closed

Making the Sides

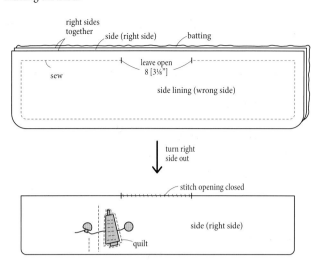

right sides together
side (right side)
batting
sew
leave open 8 [3⅛"]
side lining (wrong side)
turn right side out
stitch opening closed
side (right side)
quilt

Making Inner Pocket A

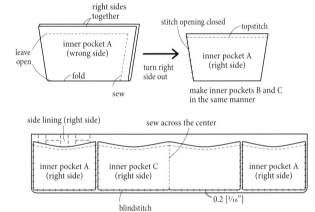

right sides together
stitch opening closed
topstitch
leave open
inner pocket A (wrong side)
turn right side out
inner pocket A (right side)
fold
sew
make inner pockets B and C in the same manner

side lining (right side)
sew across the center
inner pocket A (right side)
inner pocket C (right side)
inner pocket A (right side)
blindstitch
0.2 [1/16"]

Making the Inner Lid

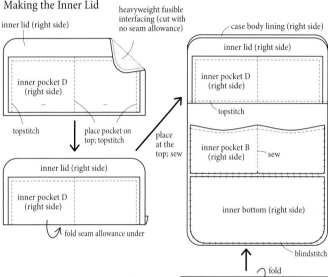

inner lid (right side)
heavyweight fusible interfacing (cut with no seam allowance)
case body lining (right side)
inner lid (right side)
inner pocket D (right side)
inner pocket D (right side)
topstitch
topstitch
place pocket on top; topstitch
place at the top; sew
inner pocket B (right side)
sew
inner lid (right side)
inner pocket D (right side)
fold seam allowance under
inner bottom (right side)
blindstitch
fold
inner bottom (wrong side)
heavyweight fusible interfacing (cut with no seam allowance)
fold

Putting the Sewing Case Together

sew the case body and the case side together

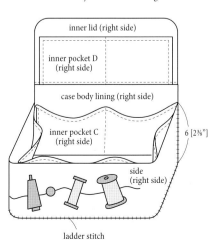

inner lid (right side)
inner pocket D (right side)
case body lining (right side)
inner pocket C (right side)
6 [2⅜"]
side (right side)
ladder stitch

Attaching the Metal Purse Frame

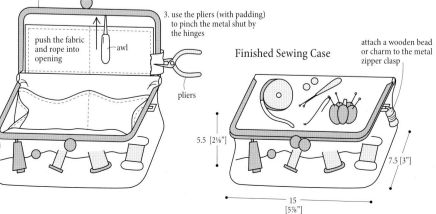

metal purse frame

1. put a thin line of glue along the metal opening
2. use the tip of an awl to push the fabric and the twisted paper rope into the opening to secure; let the glue dry
3. use the pliers (with padding) to pinch the metal shut by the hinges

push the fabric and rope into opening
awl
pliers

Finished Sewing Case

attach a wooden bead or charm to the metal zipper clasp
5.5 [2⅛"]
7.5 [3"]
15 [5⅞"]

27 Bethlehem Star Quilt ⌐····∙ p.42

► **Materials Needed**
Assorted fat quarters or scraps (appliqué)
Cotton print (background)
 – 110×270 cm [43¼" × 106¼"]
Cotton print (backing) and Batting (each)
 – 110×270 cm [43¼" × 106¼"]
Homespun (bias binding)
 – 3.5×510 cm [1⅜" ×201"]

► **Instructions**
1. Using the diagram below and the templates on the facing page, piece nine A blocks and sixteen B blocks.
2. Piece blocks A, B, C¹, C², and D together to create the quilt top.
3. With wrong sides together and batting in between, baste and quilt.
4. Bind the quilt using the bias binding to finish.

Dimensional Diagram

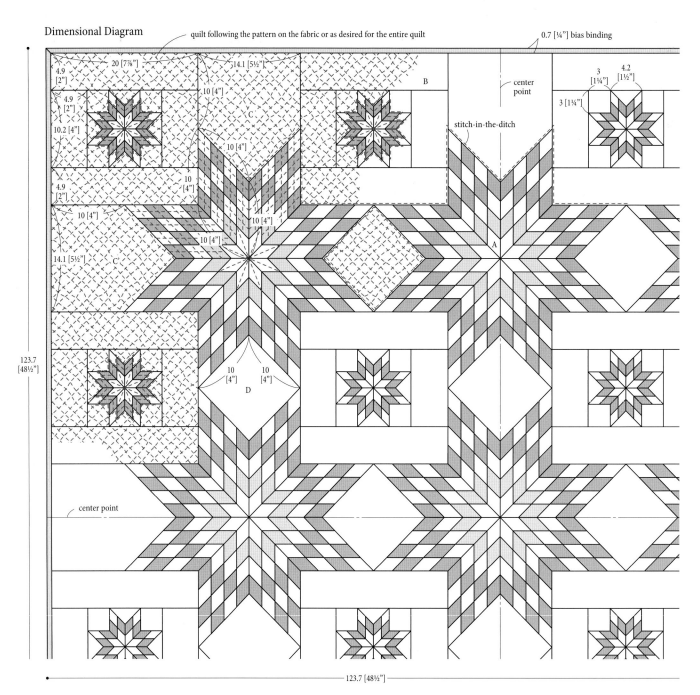

123.7 [48½"]

123.7 [48½"]

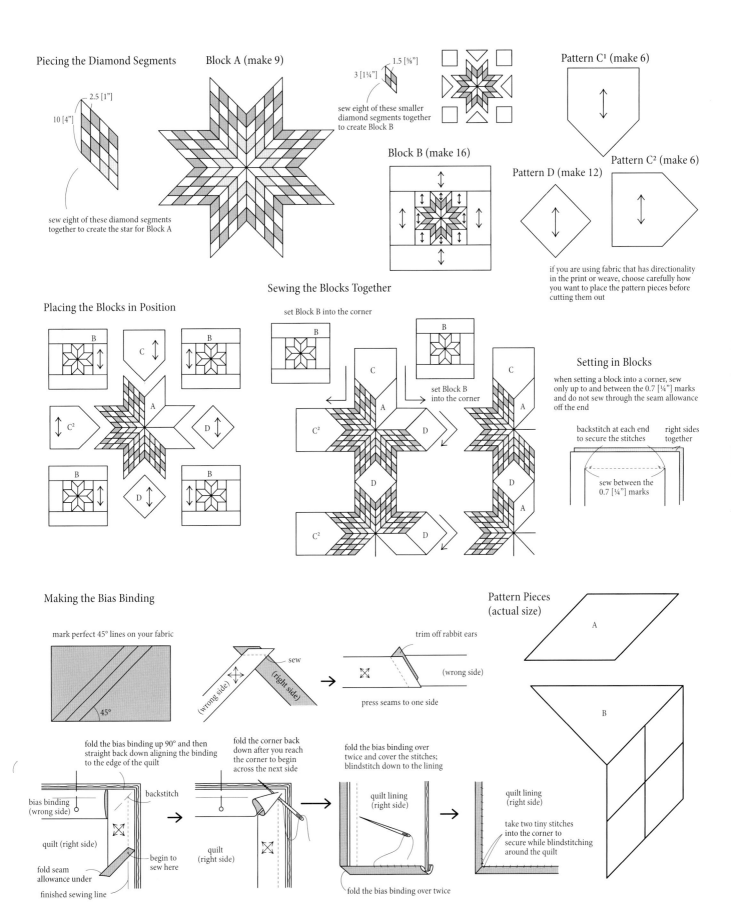

Piecing the Diamond Segments

Block A (make 9)

1.5 [⅝"]

3 [1¼"]

sew eight of these smaller diamond segments together to create Block B

Pattern C¹ (make 6)

2.5 [1"]

10 [4"]

sew eight of these diamond segments together to create the star for Block A

Block B (make 16)

Pattern C² (make 6)

Pattern D (make 12)

if you are using fabric that has directionality in the print or weave, choose carefully how you want to place the pattern pieces before cutting them out

Placing the Blocks in Position

B C B

C² A D

B D B

Sewing the Blocks Together

set Block B into the corner

B

C

C² A D

C² D

B

C

A

set Block B into the corner

D A

D A

Setting in Blocks

when setting a block into a corner, sew only up to and between the 0.7 [¼"] marks and do not sew through the seam allowance off the end

backstitch at each end to secure the stitches

right sides together

sew between the 0.7 [¼"] marks

Making the Bias Binding

mark perfect 45° lines on your fabric

45°

(wrong side) sew (right side)

trim off rabbit ears

(wrong side)

press seams to one side

fold the bias binding up 90° and then straight back down aligning the binding to the edge of the quilt

bias binding (wrong side)

quilt (right side)

fold seam allowance under

finished sewing line

backstitch

begin to sew here

fold the corner back down after you reach the corner to begin across the next side

quilt (right side)

fold the bias binding over twice and cover the stitches; blindstitch down to the lining

quilt lining (right side)

fold the bias binding over twice

quilt lining (right side)

take two tiny stitches into the corner to secure while blindstitching around the quilt

Pattern Pieces (actual size)

A

B

Baskets of Flowers Wall Quilt ┈┈┈⟶ *p.40* (enlarge template/pattern by 200% - Side B of the pattern sheet insert)

► Materials Needed
Assorted fat quarters or scraps (appliqué)
Cotton print (background)
 - 110 × 110 cm [43¼" × 43¼"]
Cotton print (backing) and Batting (each)
 - 110 × 110 cm [43¼" × 43¼"]
Homespun (bias binding)
 - 3.5 × 450 cm [1⅜" × 177"]

► Instructions
1. Using the diagram below and the patterns, ap-pliqué and embroider the quilt top.
2. With wrong sides together and batting in be-tween, baste and quilt.
3. Use the bias binding to bind the quilt.
4. Do the trapunto for the feathered quilting from the backing, rather than from the front.

Dimensional Diagram

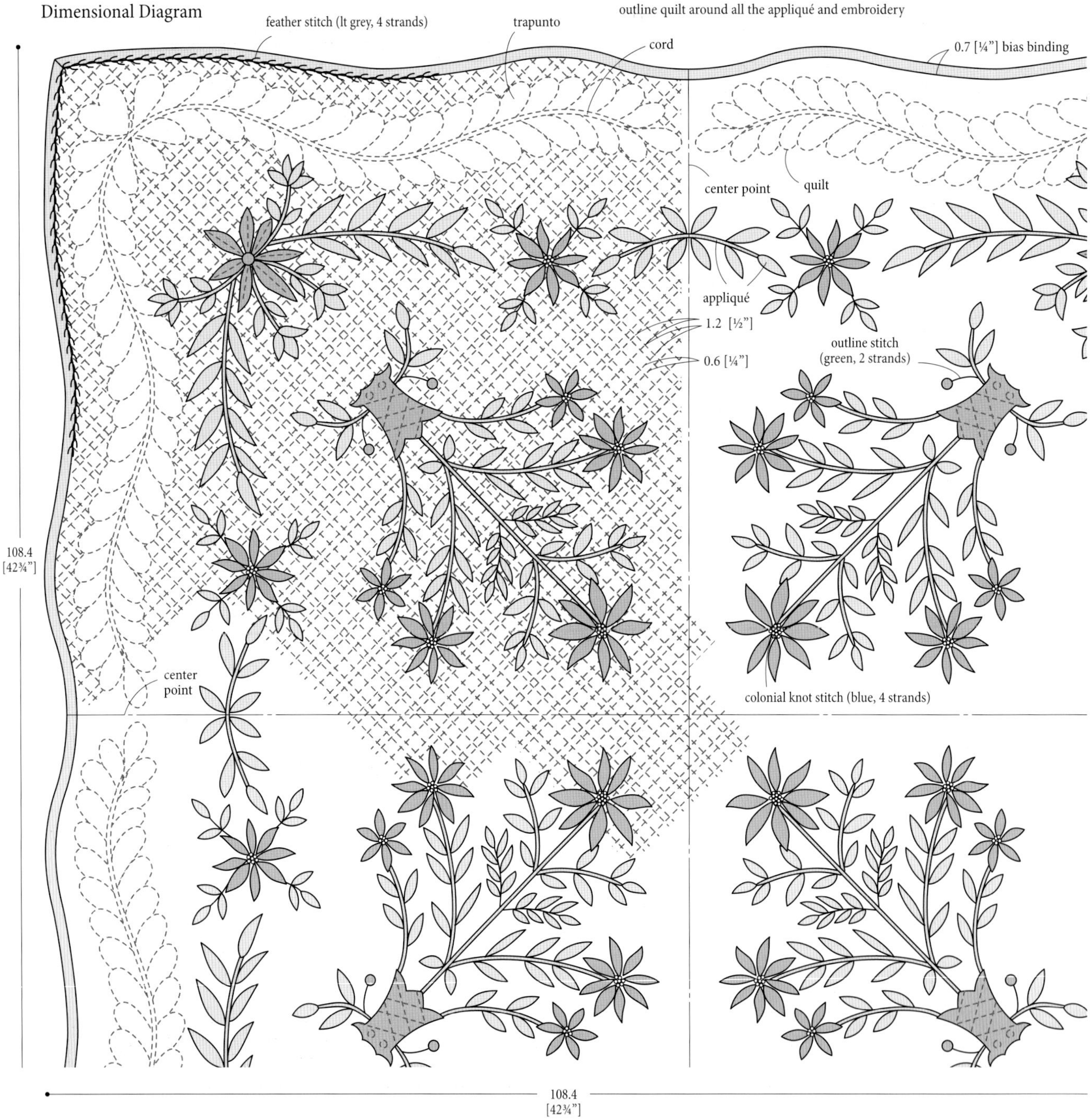

feather stitch (lt grey, 4 strands)   trapunto   outline quilt around all the appliqué and embroidery
cord
0.7 [¼"] bias binding
center point   quilt
appliqué
1.2 [½"]
0.6 [¼"]
outline stitch (green, 2 strands)
center point
colonial knot stitch (blue, 4 strands)

108.4 [42¾"]

108.4 [42¾"]

Swaying Flowers Quilt .... *p.44* (enlarge template/pattern by 200% - Side B of the pattern sheet insert)

▶ Materials Needed
Assorted fat quarters or scraps (appliqué)
Cotton print (inner border)
  – 80×140 cm [31½" × 55⅛"]
Cotton print (outer border)
  – 80×140 cm [31½" × 55⅛"]
Cotton print (backing) and Batting (each)
  – 110×300 cm [43¼" × 118"]
Cotton print (bias binding)
  – 3.5×535 cm [1⅜" ×210¾"]
Embroidery floss - colors as desired

▶ Instructions
1. Using the diagram below and the patterns and embroidery from the next two pages, appliqué and embroider center block and all of the flower blocks surrounding the center. Piece them together.
2. Using the pattern, cut out and appliqué the inner and outer border together; sew to the quilt center.
3. Make bias strips to appliqué down the stems of the flowers on top of the appliquéd seam between

the inner and outer borders to make it disappear.
4. Appliqué and embroider the rest of the flowers and leaves on the vine in the borders.
5. Bind the outside of the quilt with the bias binding to finish.

Dimensional Diagram

Appliqué/Embroidery Diagram

use a copy machine to enlarge the patterns below to 222%; use any color you desire for the embroidery stitches;
appliqué the flowers in blocks C², E², F², I², L², N² and M² in reverse

A

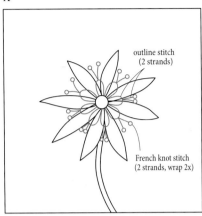

outline stitch
(2 strands)

French knot stitch
(2 strands, wrap 2x)

B

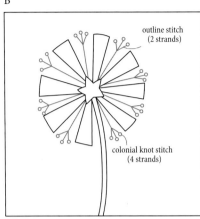

outline stitch
(2 strands)

colonial knot stitch
(4 strands)

C, C²

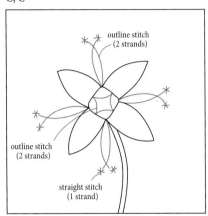

outline stitch
(2 strands)

outline stitch
(2 strands)

straight stitch
(1 strand)

D

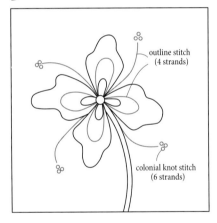

outline stitch
(4 strands)

colonial knot stitch
(6 strands)

E, E²

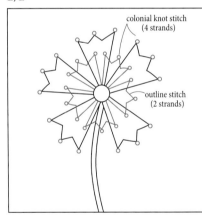

colonial knot stitch
(4 strands)

outline stitch
(2 strands)

F, F²

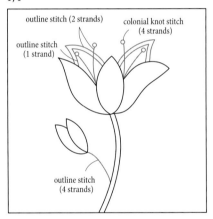

outline stitch (2 strands)

colonial knot stitch
(4 strands)

outline stitch
(1 strand)

outline stitch
(4 strands)

G

double cross stitch (2 strands)

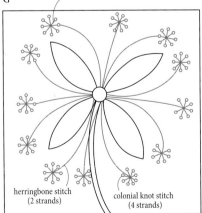

herringbone stitch
(2 strands)

colonial knot stitch
(4 strands)

H

I, I²

cross stitch (1 strand)

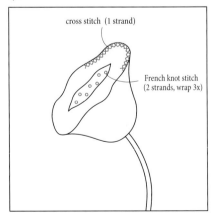

French knot stitch
(2 strands, wrap 3x)

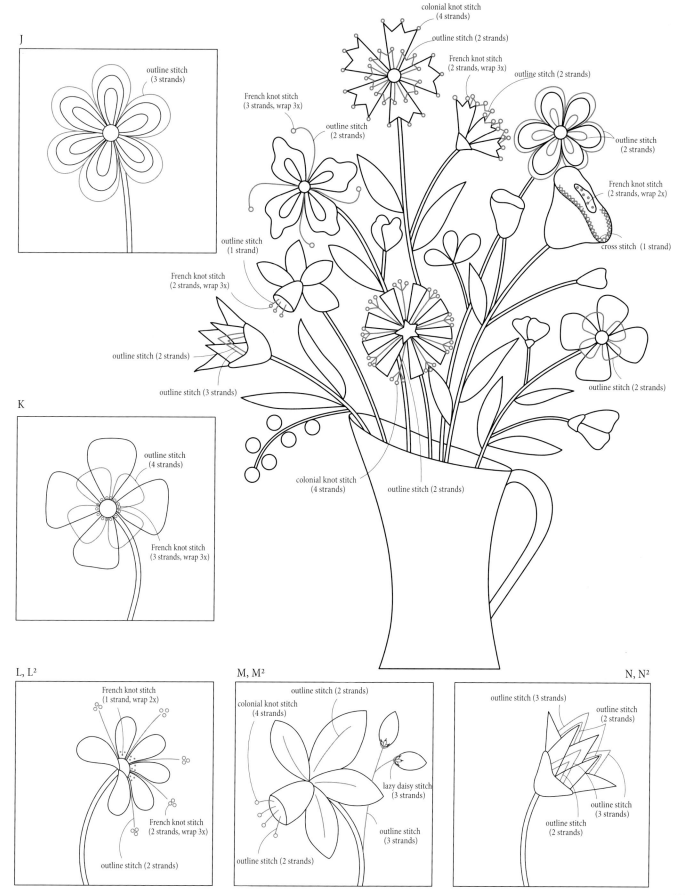

J

outline stitch
(3 strands)

colonial knot stitch
(4 strands)

outline stitch (2 strands)

French knot stitch
(2 strands, wrap 3x)

outline stitch (2 strands)

French knot stitch
(3 strands, wrap 3x)

outline stitch
(2 strands)

outline stitch
(2 strands)

French knot stitch
(2 strands, wrap 2x)

cross stitch (1 strand)

outline stitch
(1 strand)

French knot stitch
(2 strands, wrap 3x)

outline stitch (2 strands)

outline stitch (3 strands)

outline stitch (2 strands)

colonial knot stitch
(4 strands)

outline stitch (2 strands)

K

outline stitch
(4 strands)

French knot stitch
(3 strands, wrap 3x)

L, L²

French knot stitch
(1 strand, wrap 2x)

French knot stitch
(2 strands, wrap 3x)

outline stitch (2 strands)

M, M²

outline stitch (2 strands)

colonial knot stitch
(4 strands)

lazy daisy stitch
(3 strands)

outline stitch
(3 strands)

outline stitch (2 strands)

N, N²

outline stitch (3 strands)

outline stitch
(2 strands)

outline stitch
(3 strands)

outline stitch
(2 strands)

Quilt Party, Co., Ltd. (shop and school)

Quilt Party Co., Ltd.
Active Ichikawa 2F
1-23-2, Ichikawa, Ichikawa-shi,
Chiba-Ken, Japan 272-0034

http://www.quilt.co.jp (Japanese)
http://global.rakuten.com/en/store/quiltparty/ (English)

Originally from Ichikawa City in Chiba Prefecture in Japan, Yoko Saito established her quilting school and shop, Quilt Party, in 1985. She soon garnered a reputation for her masterful use and personal style of "taupe colors," as well as her beautifully precise needlework. In addition to her regular appearances on Japanese television and in magazines, she has published numerous books. In recent years, she has begun to branch out internationally, holding quilt exhibitions and workshops in countries as far as France, Italy, and Taiwan. In 2008 she commemorated thirty years of her creative career with the Yoko Saito Quilt Exhibition at the Matsuya department store in Ginza, Tokyo.

Yoko Saito

Yoko Saito's
Quilts & Projects from my Favorite Fabrics
Centenary Collection by Yoko Saito
Featuring the 20th Anniversary Centenary Collection by LECIEN

Original Title	Saito Yoko Okiniri no Nuno de Tsukuru Quilt (NV70254)
Author	Yoko Saito
First Edition	Originally published in Japan in 2014
Copyright	©2014 Yoko Saito, ©2014 Nihon Vogue-Sha; All rights reserved.
Published by:	Nihon Vogue Co., Ltd.
	3-23 Ichigaya Honmura-cho, Shinjuku-ku,
	Tokyo, Japan 162-8705
	http://book.nihonvogue.co.jp
Translation	©2016 Stitch Publications, LLC
English Translation Rights	arranged with Stitch Publications, LLC
	through Tuttle-Mori Agency, Inc.
Published by:	Stitch Publications, LLC
	P.O. Box 16694
	Seattle, WA 98116
	http://www.stitchpublications.com
Printed & Bound	KHL Printing, Singapore
ISBN	978-0-9863029-4-7
PCN	Library of Congress Control Number: 2016941787

Staff

Book Design/Layout	Wakana Takemori	Production	Kazuko Yamada, Mutsumi Yoshida, Yu Kikuchi,
Photography	Hiroaki Ishii		Keiko Sumitani, Sachiko Takenaka
	Kana Watanabe (step-by-step lessons)	Fabric/Materials	LECIEN Corporation
Styling	Terumi Inoue		http://www.lecien.co.jp/en
Pattern Illustrations	Wade Co., Ltd., (handicraft production unit)		
Editorial Assistants	Sakae Suzuki, Akiko Yoshida		
Editors	Quilts Japan Editorial		